PRAISE FOR THE LEVEYS

"You are presently engaged in work that has great prospects for bringing the inner sciences to a very wide section of people who may not under ordinary circumstances come into contact with the inner technologies of mental development and transformation."

—His Holiness the Dalai Lama

"What a beautiful book! We need so much in our world to focus on how to be instead of how to do, and your book shows the way."

—Larry Dossey, M.D., author of *Healing Words*

"*Luminous Mind* is a skillful blend of time-proven antidotes to the stress of modern life."

—Dan Goleman, Ph.D., author of *Emotional Intelligence*

"In this beautifully done book, the Leveys have skillfully woven together contemporary insights into the value and need for meditation practice in our lives with a large number of extremely evocative suggestions for making use of different ways to practice relaxation, concentration, and meditation. A real gem."

**—Jon Kabat-Zinn, Ph.D., author of *Full Catastrophe Living*
and *Wherever You Go, There You Are*, Center for
Mindfulness in Medicine, Health Care, and Society (CFM)
at the University of Massachusetts Medical Center**

"This book is an excellent primer for waking up. Practice these techniques and your life will change."

**—Richard Strozzi Heckler, Ph.D., author of
The Anatomy of Change and *Being Human at Work***

"The Leveys' book is a remarkably useful and important guide in a stressful age. Joel and Michelle free meditation from commonly held misconceptions and set it soaring—fresh and joyful—into the heart and mind of the modern-day spiritual explorer. It's meditation demystified. Pure and simple."
—**Peg Jordon, R.N., Editor In Chief,** *American Fitness Magazine*

"There is no question that relaxation and meditation are desperately needed in today's stressful society. The Leveys' book wisely emphasizes the need for relaxation and concentration exercises as skills needed to practice good meditation."
—**C. Norm Shealy, M.D., Ph.D., coauthor of** *The Creation of Health* **and** *Anatomy of the Spirit,* **Founder and Medical Director of Shealy Pain & Health Rehabilitation Institute**

"In this beautiful book, the Leveys condense two decades of study, experience, and teaching in the art of self-mastery. They make it clear that it is not stress itself that kills us but our reaction to it, and they lead the student from simple self-regulation to the heights of self-knowledge and spiritual awareness. Hopefully everyone who reads this book will make room in their life for the practices and growth program that it illustrates."
—**Dr. Elmer Green, coauthor of** *Beyond Biofeedback,* **Director of the Voluntary Control Program, Menninger Foundation**

"Perhaps the best aspect of this book is that it actually tells you what to do and how. It also explains in no-nonsense style why a certain approach is recommended and what benefit may be expected from its practice."
—**Esther-Margaret Hood,** *Hong Kong Post*

Luminous Mind

Luminous Mind

Meditation and Mind Fitness

Joel and Michelle Levey

Conari Press

This edition first published in 2006 by
Red Wheel/Weiser, LLC
With offices at:
500 Third Street, Suite 230
San Francisco, CA 94107
www.redwheelweiser.com

ISBN-10: 1-57324-296-9
ISBN-13: 978-1-57324-296-7

Library of Congress Cataloging-in Publication Data
　　Levey, Joel.
　　　　Simple meditation & relaxtion / Joel Levey and Michelle Levey.
　　　　　　p.　　cm.
　　　　Also published under title: Wisdom at work.
　　　　ISBN: 1–57324–296-9
　　　　1. Meditation.　I. Levey, Michelle.　II. Title.　III. Title: Luminous
　　　　Mind
　　　　BL627 .L48　1999
　　　　242—cd21
　　　　99–24221

Book and cover design by Donna Linden.
Typeset in Berkeley and Futura.
Cover photograph © by Corbis Corporation. All visual media © by Corbis
Corporation and/or its media providers. All Rights Reserved.

Printed in Canada
TCP

10　9　8　7　6　5　4　3　2　1

*To our many kind teachers
and to the awakening wisdom
within us all.*

CONTENTS

FOREWORD

WE LIVE IN A CULTURE WHERE STRESS has supplanted happiness as the most common state of mind. Despite the rapid growth in technology and availability of material goods, polls indicate that the typical midlife American is ten times more likely to be depressed than our grandparents were. The very things that are supposed to save time and give us the opportunity to relax and enjoy life are too often the cause of hassle and worry. The abundance of information, including the profusion of both paper and electronic mail, can be overwhelming. The realization that the Earth's resources are perilously close to depletion and that population growth is now exponential fills many of us with angst. The response to this situation has largely been one of denial and "business as usual."

Run faster, work harder, distract ourselves with television and movies, take stimulants and follow exercise regimens that are meant to relax us but often feel like one more task to fit into an overflowing schedule.

The simple truth is that we won't be able to heal the world until we can come to balance within ourselves. We can't even use our full creative potential or enjoy the blessing of intimate relationships when we are chronically worried and on overload. In the early 1900s, two Harvard physiologists, Robert M. Yerkes and John D. Dodson, discovered that a little bit of stress enhances performance, but too much stress is paralyzing. I ran a stress-disorders clinic at one of the Harvard Medical School teaching hospitals during the 1980s. Many of our clients came from the corporate world and were afraid that if they learned to relax and meditate, they would lose their edge. Most were surprised that their performance improved dramatically as they learned the kind of simple exercises that Joel and Michelle Levey describe so brilliantly in this book. Working at our edge means acquiring the tools that prevent us from going over the edge. And in the process, we learn unexpected and invaluable lessons about the nature of the human mind and the deep web of interconnections in which we live and move and evolve. As we begin to clear and focus the mind, senses become sharp and fresh, creativity explodes, we find ourselves inexplicably joyful, with the realization that life is an inexpressibly awesome and sacred gift. We learn to see with new eyes and recover the sense of wonder that we had as children.

Every spiritual leader has given similar advice. All human beings are alike. We all want to be happy. The road to happiness is a simple path, paved with actions that arise from the powerful intention to be kind and compassionate, just as we would wish others to behave toward us. A detractor once asked the first-century Rabbi Akiva to summarize the entire teaching of the Torah while standing on one foot. He replied that we should be kind to others and refrain from doing to them what we wouldn't want done to ourselves. Jesus, another first-century rabbi, gave exactly the same teaching. We know this as the Golden Rule, and while most of us would agree that it is a great idea, it is often hard to act with this degree of consciousness and caring. The true value of meditation becomes apparent over time, as kindness and caring become second nature. The fruits of practice are much more beneficial than lowered anxiety, better health, and enhanced performance. As we learn to let go of the extraneous chatter that clutters our mind, we discover that our true nature—our essential self—is actually a center of awareness, peace, and compassion. Acting with loving kindness toward others becomes our authentic state of being rather than a mere external performance.

The Lakota holy man Black Elk said, "There can never be peace between nations until we know the true peace which is in the souls of men. This comes when men realize their oneness with the universe and all its powers, and that the Great Spirit is at its center; that all things are his works, and that this center is really everywhere. It is within each of us." Joel and Michelle echo this powerful teaching of Black Elk when they remind us that "relaxation is not something that you do. It is a natural response that you allow to happen. Relaxation is what is left when you stop creating tension." When the tension melts away, we discover that we are at peace, at the center and naturally in sympathy with all creation. I used to tell my clients that they were already whole and healed—words that come from the same root as *holy*. The purpose of the tools they would learn in our clinic was to peel away the layers of stress that covered their naturally wise, peaceful, and compassionate hearts.

As I read this book, I was struck by the humble clarity with which very powerful teachings are given. I have known Joel and Michelle for a decade, admiring their strong and unwavering intention to be of service to others by sharing the wisdom they have learned from some of the most luminous spiritual teachers of our time. Their authentic, compassionate presence is always a joy to experience and a reminder that through time-tested practices, we, too, can recover peace and happiness. It was a great honor to be asked to write the Foreword to this "simple" book, which is, I believe, the most complete primer of meditation and spirituality that has ever been written.

You hold in your hand a precious jewel, a treasure with the power to transform your life and to heal the world. If it were the only book you had to study and work with for the rest of your life, it would be all that you need. Use it well and share it with others. We have all been blessed that such profound teachings from the world's great spiritual traditions have been rendered with such stunning simplicity, beauty, and grace. In a time when so many superficial books are being published, it is a rare opportunity to own a book of this depth and breadth, written in a way that allows each of us to develop our minds and hearts at exactly the pace we need.

—*Joan Borysenko, Ph.D.*

AWAKENING OUR WHOLENESS
AND FULL POTENTIAL

*A human being is part of the whole called by us
"universe," a part limited in time and space. We
experience ourselves, our thoughts, and feelings
as something separate from the rest. A kind of
optical delusion of consciousness. This delusion
is a kind of prison for us, restricting us to our
personal desires and to affection for a few
persons nearest to us. Our task must be to free
ourselves from the prison by widening our circle
of compassion to embrace all living creatures
and the whole of nature in all of its beauty. . . .
We shall require a substantially new manner
of thinking if humankind is to survive.*

—Albert Einstein

IN EACH OF OUR LIVES there have been times when we have
experienced a deeper sense of connectedness, wholeness, and
belonging than we ordinarily find. Most likely, those extraordinary moments of deeper wisdom, love, and aliveness came

unexpectedly. Pause for a moment to recall those special moments when you were most fully and joyfully alive . . . when you felt the exhilaration of performing at your best . . . when you allowed your heart to open tenderly to love and be loved . . . when you were in the flow and felt in perfect harmony with the world in which you live. Recall those quintessential moments in your life and work that stand out and sparkle . . . those times when you really helped someone or when you really allowed someone to care for you . . . those times when, for a timeless moment, you glimpsed and understood the awesomeness of creation and your belonging within it.

If we examine the qualities of our aliveness during these special times, we will probably find that our attention was wholly focused on what was happening, and that our mind and body were operating as one. These are the very qualities that are cultivated, matured, and awakened in our lives through the practices of meditation. Remembering and appreciating moments that have allowed us to know and feel life more deeply serves to remind us of what is possible. Such moments of deep recognition awaken within us an aspiration to awaken to the authenticity and fullness of who we truly are, and may further lead us to devote our lives to helping others to do the same.

Through the disciplines of meditation, we intentionally nurture and cultivate sublime qualities of vivid aliveness that are otherwise only glimpsed in moments of grace and peak experience. Generally speaking, our attention is quite scattered and our lives fragmented. Our minds and bodies seem disconnected from each other. We are often lost in our thoughts and only superficially in touch with the reality and intensity of our inner and outer experiences. How often are our minds focused, calm, clear, or open enough to discern the exquisitely profound interplay of inspiration, intuition, and revelation that are a natural, though very subtle, part of our lives? How many valuable insights, breakthrough ideas, and inspirations have danced in our mind, shimmered for a moment in lucid clarity, only to vanish because the noise level in our mindbody was simply too high to discern these subtle and sublime whispers that are an ongoing function of our human life? How many problems might be avoided if we were more grounded in our wholeness and more present—"checked in" rather than "checked out"— and more in touch with ourselves, with others, and with our surroundings?

Though our bodies are really not very different from those of our ancestors, we live in a dramatically different and infinitely more demanding world. In a single day we may be challenged to respond to more information and make more decisions than one of our ancestors faced in a lifetime! Given the accelerating rate of change and uncertainty, the immensity of personal and global crises, and the staggering variety of choices and decisions that are a part of our daily lives, is it any wonder that we often feel overwhelmed and frustrated?

With so many people in our society needlessly suffering and dying of preventable stress-related diseases, is it any wonder that so much attention is being directed to investigating practical alternatives to current ways of living and working that have been so personally and globally destructive? We in modern times have much to learn about self-knowledge and self-mastery.

It is no surprise that so many people are seeking to get in touch with deeper, life-giving forces, and that skills in meditation and relaxation are becoming recognized as vital to our peace of mind and the quality of our health, work, and relationships.

DEVELOPING THE MIND

The greatest revolution in our generation is
the discovery that human beings, by changing
the inner attitudes of their minds,
can change the outer aspects of their lives.

—William James

Our friend Charles Tart, a pioneer in the scientific research of consciousness, once said, "We don't understand the operations of our minds and hence we don't operate them very well." While many people regard the state of their mind as an unalterable "given," our research and experience have demonstrated that "upgrades" in the quality of attention, intelligence, creativity, and other mental capabilities can be dependably achieved through proper training and discipline. Motivated individuals are capable not only of improving their health but of building their "brain power," enhancing creativity, extending the length and quality of their lives, awakening greater empathy and compassion, and expanding the scope of their contribution to the world. While the multiple and complex dilemmas of modern life present multiple challenges and needs, the inner sciences of mindbody development offer a variety of profoundly practical and compassionate solutions. Once "online" and integrated into our lives, these inner skills are generative, self-reinforcing, inexpensive, portable, reliable, easily diffusible, and value-adding as they breathe life and vitality into virtually every personal and professional situation.

Regardless of the work we do or the position that we hold, our mindbody is our primary instrument. This is a truly miraculous, mysterious, and universal tool of infinite potential. With it we create and guide the use of all other tools. Yet growing up, in school, or on the job, few of us learned even the most basic skills for assuring its optimal maintenance and fine-tuning.

Consider—did your parents, teachers, health care providers, or clergy ever teach you techniques to let go of stress and tension, to harness and focus the power of your mind, or to gain deep insight through meditation? Did they themselves practice or even know of the value of these profound and useful skills? Most likely not. Lacking an education in even the basics of these skills, most of us have been virtually illiterate when it comes to the inner arts and sciences. Yet times are changing and, due to many factors, interest in these fundamental human disciplines has skyrocketed over the past thirty years.

Faced with the growing complexity of the modern marketplace we are required to think, gather, and process information, evaluate, communicate, and act at increasingly high speeds. When the situational demands—work-related, social, physiological, or psychological—exceed our capabilities to adequately respond, we experience strain and distress. Barely equipped to cope, let alone break through to higher and sustained levels of performance, many people become caught in a downward spiral that depletes their vitality and undermines their health. As a consequence, we are witnessing a growing epidemic of stress-related diseases and a host of related accidents, problems, and liabilities for business and society. The more intense our distress, the poorer the quality of the attention, judgment, creativity, and skill that we bring to our work, and the more mistakes we make. Similarly, the greater our distress level, the more likely it is that we will face conflict in our relationships or develop a life-threatening disease.

According to recent research, as much as 95% of disease is related to stress and lifestyle factors. Assistant Surgeon General William Fogey told us that two-thirds of all disability and death prior to the age of 65 is preventable—and many researchers would extend this to 85 years. So the good news is that if you really care about the quality of your life and health, you *can* make a difference!

Every moment of the day our mindbody is providing us with the information and inspiration needed to avert most of our problems. Learning to listen to this subtle stream of inner whispers gives us access to both warning signs and intuitive insights which, properly monitored and taken to heart, can cue us into recognizing the raw material for breakthroughs in creative design and problem-solving, as well as alert us to the early warning signs of accumulating stress or encroaching disease. All too often, however, the sensitive mental and physical circuitry of most individuals is so overloaded that the subtle whispers of insight and revelation that are a natural part of our life are ignored. We wait until the whispers of tension in our bodies, our relationships, and our world have become heart-wrenching screams of pain before we wake up, fully acknowledge them, and take action to restore harmony and balance. So much needless suffering could be avoided if we only learned to listen to the whispers and didn't wait for the screams!

How many moments of struggle, pain, and grief—how many billions of dollars and years of research and development—would be saved if we, as individuals and organizations, devoted more attention to refining and developing our capabilities for being truly present, and for increasing awareness through the inner technologies of mental development?

When we consider the enormous costs and damages incurred by our bodies, our relationships, our businesses, and our environment, or the multitude of valuable insights and breakthrough ideas we have missed because our inner noise level was so high, it may inspire us to learn and practice the skills presented in this book. Can we afford to not listen to the inner warnings and inspirations that may determine the course of our personal, organizational, or global future?

The disciplines of inner transformational work empower us because they are about learning to change the world from the inside out. Gandhi once said, "We must *be* the change that we want to see in our world." Speaking at Harvard University, the Dalai Lama, one of our most inspiring teachers, said:

> In this century, human knowledge is extremely expanded and developed but this is mainly knowledge of the external world.... We spend a large amount of the best human brain power looking outside—too much, and it seems we do not spend adequate effort to look within, to think inwardly.... Perhaps now that the Western sciences have reached down into the atom and out into the cosmos finally to realize the extreme vulnerability of all life and value, it is becoming credible, even obvious, that the Inner Science is of supreme importance. Certainly physics designed the bombs, biology the germ warfare, chemistry the nerve gas, and so on, but it will be the unhealthy emotions of individuals that will trigger these horrors. These emotions can only be controlled, reshaped, and rechanneled by technologies developed from successful Inner Science.

TOOLS FOR INNER WORK

This book is designed as a collection of tools for the inner work of enhancing the quality of the many dimensions of our lives. Learning to quiet the noise in the body through relaxation greatly enhances our successful practice of meditation. By practicing the skills of dynamic relaxation, we learn to master stress and recognize and reduce unproductive tensions and anxieties in our lives. By freeing ourselves from the burden of accumulated tensions and inner conflicts, we are better equipped to rest and renew ourselves, to think more clearly, keep stress from accumulating, increase our efficiency and productivity, and generally enhance our overall well-being.

On this foundation, we can begin to cultivate the disciplines of meditation presented in this book. Here you will find a wide variety of meditation practices inspired by many teachers and traditions. For simplicity, we have organized the sequence of training into five general categories: Concentration Meditation—the focused mind; Mindfulness Meditation—presence of mind; Reflective Meditation—the inquiring mind; Creative Meditation—the transformative mind; and Heart-Centered Meditation—the mind of loving-kindness.

Approached in this way, meditation techniques enable us to build the power and peace of mind needed to awaken insight and understanding. Awakening and embodying wisdom is the true goal of meditation. This awakening is necessary to consciously recognize and transform the harmful or unproductive patterns of our lives, and to consciously strengthen the mind's full potential for wisdom, love, power, and creative compassion. As we develop a deeper understanding, our appreciation for the true nature and potential of ourselves and others grows; inner and outer conflicts diminish; and we become more joyful, creative, and effective in living life, helping others, and stewarding the world.

Quality relationships are both the foundation and the fruit of meditation practice: by reducing the turbulence in our outer lives, we reduce the turbulence and stress in our minds and bodies. When our body is relaxed and our mind is calm and clear, we are better able to live mindfully, think and listen deeply, and awaken greater wisdom and compassion through our meditations, which in turn improve the quality of relationships.

At the end of the book we have included a reference for resources to support your continued inquiry and learning, and to offer additional ideas and strategies for exploring the many streams of these practices. We have also provided an index of the various meditations described in this book so that you may easily find and refer to specific ones.

RELAXATION, PEAK PERFORMANCE, AND BEYOND

This book is a mental-fitness manual for everyone interested in learning methods to enhance their health and performance, master stress, and deepen their appreciation of life. It is also a handbook for those who wish to understand and master these skills in order to teach them to others or to equip themselves to make a greater contribution to the world. Whatever your motivation, you will find that the ideas and techniques in this collection have been presented with an emphasis on their practical applications in our busy, modern lives, while preserving a sense of the depth and sacredness traditionally associated with the inner arts of personal development. We suggest that you ponder these ideas with your intellect, contemplate their meaning and value in your heart, and test and confirm their profound practicality in the laboratory or the playing field of your daily life, work, and relationships.

If you are primarily interested in physical relaxation or in learning to stay centered, calm, and focused amid the chaos of daily life, you will find many of these techniques highly effective. If exploring the nature and potential of your mindbody is important to you, there are methods to ripen that understanding. If improving your mental and physical performance or building healthier and more harmonious relationships is of significance to you, there are many strategies that will help you in these arenas as well. And if you approach this inquiry with a heartfelt sense of devotion, a sincere yearning to deepen your spiritual insight and to awaken within yourself a sense of universal compassion that empowers you to be of greater service to others, many of these methods will serve as a vehicle to transform and open your heart-mind to new dimensions of wisdom, wonder, love, and inner strength.

FIELD-TESTED WISDOM AND METHODS

Over the past thirty years, we have had the rare opportunity to study and practice closely with great teachers from many of the world's religious and contemplative traditions. From these remarkable men and women we have learned thousands of effective techniques for developing the full potential of the human mindbody. In many cases these methods have been practiced, cherished, and preserved with inspiring results for millennia.

Many of these revered masters and respected researchers of the inner arts and sciences encouraged us to carry what they had taught us back into our world. We have treasured what they shared with us and with their guidance and blessings, have shared what we have learned with tens of thousands of people around the globe. Following the examples of many of our teachers, our lives have been blessed with times of travel, teaching, consulting, and service work in the world, and with times of intensive, quiet cloistered retreat. Over the years, we have each spent a total of about three years in intensive silent meditation retreats and have maintained a discipline of a daily meditation practice, both of which have deeply influenced and guided our work in the world.

This book contains a distillation of over a hundred methods that we have found personally and professionally effective. The contemporary renaissance of interest in matters of mental health and fitness, spirit, and consciousness has brought these methods of relaxation and meditation out of caves, monasteries, and remote cultures into medical centers, meeting rooms, research institutions, and the mainstream of modern life. These skillful methods have been scientifically studied and demonstrated to be highly effective for enhancing health and mental and physical performance, awakening creativity, and tapping the life-giving and vitality-enhancing forces of our lives. They are also effective antidotes to the epidemic of stress-related diseases, anxiety, hostility, loneliness, depression, dysfunctional behavior, and existential yearning that plague our complex and rapidly changing world.

Over the past three decades we have relied upon these inner arts as primary tools in our work in several fields: as mental fitness coaches for world-class and Olympic champions and corporate peak performers; researchers investigating the nature of human consciousness; clinicians teaching psychophysical self-optimization skills to adults, children, and staff in leading medical centers; organization design and creativity consultants to leaders in business and industry; graduate faculty for programs in medicine and psychology; biocybernautic instructors for a pioneering program with elite teams of U.S. Army Special Forces troops; counselors for people facing terminal illness or grieving the loss of a loved one; and coaches and friends to many people seeking to live in a more integrated, authentic, and spirited way and to be more effective in helping others realize the same quality in their own lives.

THE SPIRIT OF THESE TEACHINGS

We hope that you will read this book in the spirit of one of our corporate clients, a woman with sincere interest but little formal knowledge of the contemplative arts. We met her in an airport one day and she said, "Hey! I read your book, and I want you to know that by reading your book I feel like I have met your teachers!" We both burst into tears. Many of these remarkable teachers, with whom we devoted years of traveling and studying, spoke in foreign languages and their translators painstakingly passed their teachings and instructions along to us. Many a late night we have sat talking with these kind and patient teachers and translators, clarifying our questions and the fine technical points of their remarkable meditation instructions. With their blessings, guidance, and encouragement we have gradually come to find ourselves often in the role of teacher and translator for those not fortunate enough to meet these great teachers in person.

One point we want to make is that we have received so much from so many incredible people, many of whom were, in a way, the last of their species on this planet because the sacred vessels of their wisdom cultures have been destroyed. They gave of their wisdom to us, saying, "Please cherish these gifts. Keep the spirit of these teachings alive. Pass them on to the generations to come"—and they knew we would. Holding lineages of teachings that have been cherished and preserved for millennia, these teachers have offered a living transmission of the stream of ancient wisdom into modern times. In recent years, many of our remarkable teachers have died. We, and others as fortunate as us, are left holding the basket of their precious teachings. So for us to weave together this small basket of teachings and to be able to pass it on to you is really a great privilege. If in some way this book contributes to the awakening of the wisdom and creative compassion that our teachers so inspiringly embodied and taught, then our intentions in writing it will have been fulfilled.

CROSSING THE THRESHOLD

When we embarked on a yearlong silent meditation retreat in 1988, the Venerable Gen Lamrimpa, the Tibetan lama leading the retreat, once said to us, "As you go deeper and deeper into this practice of meditation, gradually you will become aware of many dimensions of reality that you previously were unaware of." We welcome you to this threshold, and we pray that as you take these methods, principles, and teachings to heart and apply them to your life, the horizons of your own understanding will continue to expand in an endlessly awe-inspiring way.

HOW TO GET THE MOST FROM THIS BOOK

The challenges of millennia and the inspiration of the human spirit have given rise to thousands of techniques of relaxation and meditation. Each of these methods is effective for building our positive strengths and overcoming the factors that block the flow of our life-giving energies. In this book you will find the distillation of those methods we have found to be most widely conducive for enhancing the quality of health and performance, building confidence and self-esteem, mastering distress, and awakening creativity, compassion, power, and peace of mind.

We suggest that you consider this book as an investment portfolio offering you a wide range of options. Your return will depend largely upon the sincerity and continuity of your investment of attention and aspiration. Though the methods are priceless, you must make a personal investment in them in order to discover and call forth their power and sweetness. The greater your personal investment in taking these principles to heart, the greater your return and the more you will have to offer to the world.

There are three steps in mastering these techniques. Reading or hearing about them is the first step. Contemplating and thinking about their meaning, value, and application in your daily life is the second step. Taking the meaning and value to heart and directly applying them to your life is the third step. All three steps are important in discovering the power and profundity of each technique. Though benefits may be immediately apparent, the real fruits of these methods will only emerge gradually as you cultivate them with sustained effort. As your practice deepens, the fruits will grow sweeter and your appreciation of life as a continuously improving learning process will grow.

How long will it take to master a technique? How long would it take you to learn to master the flute or cello? The key to all learning is personal commitment and discipline. While books, tapes, and teachers are invaluable, ultimately it will be your own diligence that will assure your success. Have faith in your ability to tap the life-giving forces available to you. The beauty, pain, and uncertainties in your life and in the world will provide a continual reminder of the vital importance of practicing these skills.

Each of the chapters on the different forms of meditation begins with an introduction and a description of guidelines for using the methods contained in that section, followed by the practices themselves. As you read, we encourage you to note those ideas and exercises that seem to speak most directly to your needs and interests. This chart will help you identify the techniques in this book that speak most directly to specific issues you may wish to attend to in your practice.

If you are interested in . . .	Experiment with techniques on these pages
Flow state, peak performance, and achieving peak performance	41–47, 66, 69, 73–74, 83, 88, 90, 127, 135, 158, 176, 190
Enhancing creativity, innovative thinking, and intuition	41–47, 67, 69, 70, 90, 124-134, 153-190, 214, 243
Self-empowerment	41-47, 83, 90, 127, 135, 173, 174, 176, 186, 190, 195, 197, 214
Mastering attention	63, 64, 65, 66, 67, 69, 70, 73–74, 83, 84, 90, 103, 106, 178, 190, 206
Mastering physical distress (headaches, muscle pain, aches, tics, etc.)	78, 88, 158, 214
Mastering mental distress (anxiety, worry, intrusive or repetitive thoughts, etc.)	47, 63, 67, 73–74, 90–102, 103, 106, 124, 125, 186, 190
Mastering emotional and autonomic distress (hypertension, migraine headaches, eating disorders, addictive behaviors, etc.)	88, 103, 120, 135, 195, 197, 206, 214
Opening the heart: awakening love and compassion	41–47, 108, 127, 135, 193–220
Strategies for working with pain and enhancing healing	41–47, 64, 88, 158, 174, 176, 214
Tapping the life-giving forces of the human spirit	41–47, 69, 70, 73–74, 90, 127, 128, 134, 153, 158, 174, 176, 178, 186, 190, 214, 243

Once you have identified them, put them into practice by reading them slowly and thoughtfully. Then proceed step by step to get the feeling behind the words. You may find it helpful to have a friend read the exercise to you, or to record it in your own voice to replay at your leisure. Or you may feel inspired to change our terminology to better suit your own style or beliefs. As your familiarity with a technique grows, you will learn to mentally progress through its various stages without needing to read or listen to the instructions. Though at first you may mentally talk yourself through an exercise, gradually cultivate the skill to move through the method as a progression of shifts in awareness, a series of mental images or feelings, rather than mere words and concepts.

THREE FOUNDATIONS OF INNER DEVELOPMENT

The classical teachings on meditation exist within a larger body of spiritual teachings that span all of the dimensions of our lives. Universally, the foundation of meditation practice is rooted in developing harmonious relationships with the world around us. When we are out of harmony with our world and with those who share it, that disharmony is reflected within us as tension, distraction, confusion, frustration, anger, or enmity. When the mind is dominated by these disturbing "mental poisons," and the body is flooded with their associated biochemical analogues, it is virtually impossible to bring enough balance to the mind to engage in any fruitful meditation. If you are really intent upon developing yourself, then your first step is to begin to make peace and find harmony in relationship to your world. The practice of ethics, morality, and "right relations" not only benefits others but, in the long run, helps us create the causes for inner peace that we long for. The stronger this foundation, the more profound and fruitful will be our meditation practice.

As Vietnamese poet and Buddhist teacher Thich Nhat Hanh reminds us, the world is both wonderful and terrible: there is considerable injustice and tragic suffering. Making peace with the world is not to look away from these heartbreaking circumstances, but to have the courage to witness suffering with compassion and understanding. Only then will we have the insight necessary to respond with wisdom and effectiveness.

Though living in accord with the Golden Rule is enough to transform our lives, a second foundation is necessary to really establish a meditation practice. As outer turbulence subsides, we are left to the inner work of reducing the turbulence within ourselves. Taking the first step, we focus within our body and begin to recognize the ways we armor ourselves with unnecessary tension. Then, applying the principles of kindness and merciful compassion to ourselves, we learn ways to relax and to release the unnecessary tension we carry in our body. Looking ever more deeply, we find that physical tension is tied to the inner tension and turmoil of our mind-emotions. So, as you see, the practice of kindness and compassion—inner and outer—is really the ground of meditation.

As we learn to open blocked energy, release tension, and come to rest more at ease in our body, we are better able to engage in the inner work of enhancing the power of our mindful attention. This opens the next doorway to meditation: the development of concentration. Developing concentration transforms mental dullness into mental stability, distraction into vivid mental clarity. Along the way we also develop the strength of our mindfulness and vigilance—so necessary to keeping our meditation focused and on track. As a result of this inner transformational work, we are able to bring a calm intensity to whatever we do, and this powerful peace of mind can then be carried into our lives, relationships, and any other meditation practices we may engage in.

These three foundations—"right relations," relaxation, and meditation—create outer and inner harmony and a focused presence of mind. Together they support the awakening of wisdom and compassion—the real goal of our practice. Profound insight arises. We see that when our body is at ease in its natural state and our mind isn't being unnecessarily churned, the mind is calm, peaceful, and vividly clear. And when the mind is peaceful, present, and undisturbed, the world we behold is one of wholeness. We understand that the natural state of our relationships is that of deep interdependence, completely empty of isolation and separateness.

As our understanding of all these factors emerges, we realize the true measure and test of meditation training. This is found in a spiritual maturity that results from taming the mind's fixations; eliminating such basic malaise as selfishness, greed, and hatred; deepening insight into the nature of reality; and the awakening of a growing concern for the well-being of others. Meditative powers and insights are honestly of little value if they don't help us to do these things.

THE DANCE OF MASTERY AND MYSTERY

Nobody...knows what a single thing is. It is a great and wonderful mystery to us all that anything is or that we are. And whenever anyone says, "I don't know how anything came to be," or "God made everything," they are simply pointing to the feeling of the Mystery—of how

everything is, but nobody knows what it really is, or how
it came to be. . . . If you will remember every day to feel
the Mystery, and if you will remember that you are more
than what you look like, and if you will remember to be
the Mystery itself, then you will be happy every day.

—the words of a young child

This book invites—and challenges—you to learn to dance
with Mystery and mastery in your life. The inner alchemy
that weds mastery to Mystery is sometimes described as the
marriage of Earth and Heaven, as the harmonizing of yang
and yin or the creative and the receptive, as merging mascu-
line and feminine, or as balancing intellect and intuition.
True mastery is realized only when our discipline has been
so wholehearted that it carries us to the threshold where, to
go any further, we must surrender to Mystery. The union of
mastery and Mystery is a path toward wholeness, a dynamic
state of being as natural as inhalation and exhalation, the
pulse and stillness of each heartbeat, or the striding, balanced rhythm of our two feet carrying us along life's path.

Through the practice of relaxation and meditation we
increase our mastery as well as our capacity to sustain the
intensity of Mystery's natural grace. We participate in the
self-renewing revelation of creation described by the great
mystics of the world, and we drink from the wellsprings of
our deepest nature at the heart of all creation. As our meditative insights deepen, we unify mastery and Mystery and
open the inner depths of our being to discover a stream of
inspiration rising forth and flowing through us as a blessing
to our lives and the lives of all we meet. Mastery reveals
Mystery and is truly guided by Mystery, and each breath
becomes a journey weaving our countless dimensions into a
unified wholeness.

ONE
WHAT IS MEDITATION?

*Meditation opens the mind to the greatest mystery
that takes place daily and hourly; it widens the
heart so that it may feel the eternity of time and
infinity of space in every throb; it gives us a life
within the world as if we were moving about
in paradise; and all these spiritual deeds take
place without any refuge into a doctrine, but
by the simple and direct holding fast to the
truth which dwells in our innermost beings.*

—Shunryu Suzuki Roshi

AT THE HEART OF EACH GREAT RELIGIOUS TRADITION is a
wisdom school of transformational contemplative teachings.
While the exoteric religious teachings provide many guidelines and examples for conducting one's daily life, the more
psychological and meditative teachings of the esoteric
schools have provided practitioners throughout the ages
with practical and systematic guidelines for transforming

ourselves and fully developing our human potential. Meditation techniques are best understood as methods of mental and spiritual training.

Today, meditation techniques are undergoing a secular revival as our state oracle of science discovers and proclaims the benefits of meditation as a remedy to the epidemic stress of modern life. In the last ten years, it has become increasingly common to find the practice of meditation encouraged in high-level corporate creativity sessions, in locker rooms, during coffee breaks, before and after work, prior to academic tests, before athletic competition, and even in military maneuvers. With the use of relaxation, imagery, attention training, or meditation many people are being introduced to powerful and highly effective mental technologies of personal transformation that have been the cherished and often secret practices of many ancient traditions.

This trend has sometimes been attributed as a shift from left-brain to right-brain thinking, or as the meeting of Eastern and Western values in life. For our purposes here, let's consider meditation as a skillful means for moving from the pain of our personal and planetary fragmentation toward the direct intuitive understanding of our wholeness and potential as human beings.

Contemporary psychology and medicine regard the contemplative traditions as a rich source of skills for mastering attention, promoting health and stress resilience, reducing pain, awakening creativity, and building the power of positive emotions such as empathy, patience, joy, and loving-kindness. Thousands of research studies have documented the benefits of these methods, and many centers for medicine and peak performance have integrated them. Acknowledging that most people have little control over their attention and have few effective skills for developing their mental health and emotional intelligence, the contributions of meditation training are receiving more and more attention.

INTEGRATING ACTIVE AND QUIET MIND SKILLS

One way to understand meditation practices is that they help us integrate and develop the dynamic synergy of both our active or creative mind skills, and our quiet or receptive mind skills. Insights and inspirations emerge first as subtle, formless impressions, gossamer-like and transparent—so elusive that they are easily ignored. If our "quiet mind skills" are keen enough, however, even the subtlest emerging insights will be noticed and drawn into awareness. Once these impressions are brought onto the screen of conscious awareness, our "active mind skills" come into play, shaping and developing them into thoughts, images, and intentions that can be communicated to others and guide our action and work in the world.

The "active mind skills" are the tools of our intellect and reasoning. They include intention or will, thinking and reasoning, and our faculty of creative imagination. These skills each play a role in shaping or transforming information through the power of intention. They also give form and meaning to the flow of information and the chaos of our experience by creating order through the power of thought and imagination. The active mind skills are vital to organizing and expressing our inner knowing, insights, feelings, and intentions, and for translating our thoughts and visions into action. Active mind skills help us to make sense of both internal mental experience and the perceived experience from our outer world, and to communicate our understanding to others.

The "quiet mind skills" represent a domain of powerful mental functions that are complementary to and essential for the effective use of the "active mind skills." Quiet mind skills are primarily attentive or receptive mental functions that gather information through the faculty of mindful attention, sensing, and feeling. These involve the qualities of receptivity, "being," or presence, in contrast to the creativity, or "doing" nature of the active mind skills. By way of analogy, the active mind skills can be compared to the forms and patterns of matter or clouds that we can see or touch, and the dynamic forces of wind, water, or electromagnetism that shape them. The subtler mental functions and brain states associated with the quiet mind are more "transparent," like the sheer presence of the sky—vast in scope, clear, and open. For this reason they are rarely recognized, and seldom fully developed. Their level of development, however, determines the coherence and power of all other mental functions. Critically important to accessing and expressing a deeper quality of wisdom and presence in our lives, the depth of our quiet mind skills determines our capacity for coping with intensity and complexity. They also provide access to the subtle revelations of intuitive insight so vital to breakthroughs in creativity and innovation, and are the key to integrating both intellect and intuition.

Consciously or unconsciously, all the great scientists and sages of the world have tapped the quiet mind skills as the access states necessary to discover the "universal organizing principles" that have inspired and guided the development of humanity throughout the ages. By allowing us to focus our attention more deeply, they enable us to discover a more fundamental wisdom that reveals insight into the nature of our innermost being and the world in which we live. In this way, the quiet mind skills awaken our sensitivity to life-giving forces that are expressed as universal values, such as wisdom, compassion, heartfelt appreciation, and wonder.

Though few people have received any formal training in either the active or quiet mind skills, all of us, to some degree, rely on these faculties to make sense of our experience, and to organize our thinking and working. In fact, the quality of our work, communication, thinking, creativity, and health are intimately related to how fully we have developed the synergy of these two kinds of capabilities. The different styles of meditation practice found in this book are designed to provide you with the kind of "mental fitness" training that will help you cultivate your capacity to integrate both of these essential domains.

THE THREEFOLD GOAL OF MEDITATION

Meditation practice is undertaken with a threefold goal. The first is to discover and transform the limiting habits of mind that block our full potential. The second is to actively culti-vate and bring more fully alive our potential for wisdom, creative intelligence, calm intensity, loving-kindness, and compassion. Third, when really taken to heart, we practice with the motivation not only to free ourselves from limita-tions and to awaken to our own true nature and potential, but in order to be more effective in helpings others realize their full potential as well. After all, how much satisfaction will we find if we are free from our problems yet everyone else around us is still suffering? We work on ourselves because we understand that it will make us a better parent, a better friend, a more sensitive and creative human being contributing to our community. Our inner work is an offer-ing to the world. What greater offering can we make?

Choices in a meditator's life are very simple:
Do those things that contribute to your awareness,
and refrain from those things that do not.

—Sujata

FIVE CATEGORIES OF MEDITATION TECHNIQUES

A person well versed in inner science traditions has access to a veritable apothecary of meditative antidotes to disturbing mind states, as well as to potent methods for enhancing and developing wholesome and helpful states of mind. Mastering our mind in these ways, we will inevitably develop mastery over our physical and verbal expressions and our relationship with the world.

There are thousands of meditation techniques from many different traditions, but all could be classified as belonging to either one or a combination of five categories:

1. Concentration Meditation

2. Mindfulness Meditation

3. Reflective Meditation

4. Creative Meditation

5. Heart-Centered Meditation

Concentration meditation is the foundation for all other kinds of meditation. Through the power of concentration we build our capacity to overcome distraction and to sustain mental focus. The power of a scattered mind is very limited. But like a stream of water that can be channeled to make it more forceful and produce hydroelectric power, we can make the mind a more powerful instrument by developing a small seed of one-pointed mindfulness into "concentration power." In classical meditation texts, this one-pointedness of mind developed through the energy of concentration is called *samadhi*, which literally means "to establish, to make firm."

The power of a concentrated mind can be focused effectively to enhance and deepen insight into other meditative themes or goals. To understand how this works, compare the illuminating capacity of the diffuse and scattered beam of a ten-watt incandescent lightbulb to the penetrating, diamond-like precision of a ten-watt laser beam. Such is the difference in illuminating power of the concentrated mind to the ordinary, scattered, and fragmentary flow of attention that most of us bring to everyday living. By learning how to bring the stream of our attention into a laser-like beam of one-pointed concentration, we can train the mind to become a highly useful instrument for penetrating into and investigating the nature of reality. A concentrated mind is also the precursor of great bliss and the prerequisite for the development of psychic abilities.

Whatever technique of meditation you are practicing, it is necessary to have the ability to place your attention on the object of meditation and hold it there without distraction. With patience and practice, your mind will become calmer, more powerful, and able to apply itself to any task with precision and understanding. Any object or activity can be used for the specific development of concentration. The same basic principle, however, always applies, no matter which form of meditation you are practicing: whenever your mind wanders, simply return it—again and again—to the object of your meditation.

Mindfulness meditation emphasizes the cultivation of a receptive, choiceless quality of mindful attention toward whatever arises in the sphere of our experience. At those times in our lives when we were rapt in wonder gazing into the depths of the night sky, listening intently, marveling at the beauty of nature, or wholeheartedly listening for the answer to our heart's prayer, we have naturally experienced this type of meditation. Traditionally, the practices of insight or *vipassana* meditation, *zazen, dzogchen,* Mahamudra, choiceless awareness, self-remembering, and prayer of the heart are associated with this category of meditation. Mindfulness meditation strengthens our sense of wonder and appreciation, enabling us to effortlessly, precisely, and carefully attend to the totality of our experience unfolding moment to moment.

The interplay of concentration and mindfulness meditation allows us to develop the capacity to examine and intuitively understand the deep forces within our ordinary experience. The penetrating insight that develops can then be systematically applied to investigating the very subtle interplay between the phenomena we perceive and the nature of our own mind as the perceiver. As we investigate our participation in the pervasive and dynamic interrelatedness of everything, we will come to sense ourselves as intimately related to and co-creative with the world of our experience.

The practice of reflective or analytical meditation is like disciplined thinking: choosing a theme, question, or topic of contemplation we focus our reflection, or analysis, upon it. When our attention wanders to other thoughts, we return to our chosen topic. Traditionally, reflective meditation is employed to gain insight into the meaning of life, death, interrelationships, and social conscience, or to come to a conclusive insight regarding some key idea in science, philosophy, or scripture. Following our analysis through, we arrive at a conclusion. This, in turn, gives rise to a strong sense of faith or conviction.

In our day-to-day life and work, reflective meditation provides us with a powerful and effective tool for focusing our attention upon personal or professional questions in order to discover a creative solution or breakthrough insight. Reflective meditation also helps us to understand the issues or inner conflicts that may arise during the practice of other meditations.

Creative meditation enables us to consciously cultivate and strengthen specific qualities of mind. Patience, appreciation, sympathetic joy, gratitude, love, compassion, fearlessness, humility, tenderness, and other qualities associated with aspects of nature, Divinity, or the natural world are among the attributes that are most commonly cultivated. Creative meditations invite us to actively nurture these strengths of character by thinking, speaking, and acting "as though" these qualities are more fully alive within us.

Heart-centered meditation helps us to awaken the radiance of our loving-kindness and compassion. They deepen our empathy and forgiveness, and teach us to live in kinder ways. They begin first with ourselves, and then open the circle of our compassion to embrace all living beings. They draw inspiration from each of the other meditations: focus and the power of peace from concentration; deep listening and presence from mindfulness meditation; insight into the nature of suffering and a sense of interrelatedness from reflective meditation; imaginative resourcefulness and skill from creative meditation.

Properly understood, all of these approaches to meditation are interrelated and mutually enhancing. Many practices draw inspiration from a variety of meditation styles and could be included in several categories. While the intricacies of these interrelationships are beyond the scope of this book, it should be clear to you that the contemplative traditions offer us the inner technology necessary to fulfill virtually any developmental aspiration we may have. Meditation allows us to go beyond words and mental concepts in order to know the true nature and reality of ourselves and our world directly.

TWO
GUIDELINES FOR DEVELOPING MEDITATION SKILLS

CLEAN AND CLEAR SPACE

CREATE A SPECIAL SPACE for yourself, either a room or a corner, and use it only for your meditation and heartfelt study or contemplation. Put in this space only those things that help your meditation. Find a comfortable seat for yourself. Arrange in a pleasing way the pictures and objects that energize the qualities of heart and mind you are trying to nurture. Keep the space clean and clear, as though you were always expecting a special guest. Enter it with respect, and be uplifted and refreshed by its peace, beauty, and healing qualities.

MINDING THE BODY

In general, you will find it helpful to precede your quiet sitting meditation with at least a brief period of mindful stretching, tai chi, yoga, or gentle exercise. This will help you to build energy and focus your attention. At times you may find that your mind is simply too agitated to begin with quiet sitting meditation and you will gain much greater benefit from a session of walking or moving meditation such as Concentration While Walking (page 73), Doing What You Love to Do (page 83), or Mindful Walking (page 106).

For sitting meditation, whether you sit cross-legged, in a chair, or kneel with a meditation bench is largely a matter of style and preference. Experiment and see what works best for you. It is especially important to sit comfortably, with your spine straight and your body upright and relaxed. Sitting in this way, it will be much easier to remain alert. Sit naturally and at ease, and avoid forcing your body into uncomfortable postures. Your eyes can either be gently closed or softly open—though practicing with them softly open will reduce the tendency to doze off and can help you to carry a meditative presence over into other activities. With practice you will learn to bring a meditative mind to every activity, whether sitting, standing, walking, or lying down.

RELEASE PHENOMENA

In meditation, as you begin to relax, it is quite common to experience what are called "release phenomena." These may include jerking or quivering of the body as you are falling asleep, gurgling of the stomach, tingling feelings or numbness, memories, mental images, inner sounds, or other perceptual changes.

Release phenomena are common indicators that your practice of relaxation or meditation is becoming effective in dissolving deeply imbedded mental, emotional, and physical holding patterns. The best way to deal with these experiences is to simply allow them to arise, unfold, and dissolve without distracting your attention.

With practice, you will become aware of the subtle physical, emotional, and mental states that are the indicators of progressively deeper levels of relaxation and meditation. Eventually, your reservoirs of accumulated stress will be drained, allowing you to feel lighter, clearer, and better able to handle the challenges of daily life more effectively and with greater patience and understanding.

RELAXED YET ALERT

For most of us, our experience of deep relaxation lacks awareness and is at best dull and dreamlike. And at the very height of alertness we are the complete opposite of relaxed, experiencing physical tension and mental agitation. Both of these extremes are far from the relaxed yet alert, calm delight of meditative equipoise. A classical analogy talks of tuning a stringed musical instrument: If the strings are too tight or too loose the sound is not very pleasant. Similarly, to find the sweet notes in meditation, it is necessary to find a dynamic balance between being overly alert and overly relaxed. The first extreme creates physical and mental tightness and eventually leads to distraction. The other end of the continuum creates dullness and heaviness that usually leads to sleep.

Especially in the beginning, much of your session might be spent finding this balance, bringing the mind back from dazed distraction or dullness to a state of relaxed alertness. Eventually, you will become familiar with this state of being. During your meditation sessions you will be able to be deeply relaxed as well as extremely lucid, and in daily life you will find that your view of the way things are will be less conditioned and obstructed. With this deepening understanding, you will be better able to optimize your response to the challenges and opportunities of each moment with more creative and compassionate attitudes, words, and actions.

DYNAMIC RELAXATION: HAVE MERCY

As we were about to enter into a long meditation retreat, we visited one of our special teachers. With intense and tender concern, he took us by the hand, looked deeply into our eyes and said, "If you wish to be successful in your meditation practice, the most important thing is to remember to stay relaxed! If you get tense and try too hard, it will only create problems." Dynamic relaxation is a first step in opening to our wholeness, our full potential, and to the world. As you learn to relax and to release unnecessary tension, the physical vitality, mental clarity, calm, centered strength, and emotional well-being which are fundamental to the human spirit, will naturally and effortlessly arise. The tensions we hold in our day-to-day lives are, in many cases, armoring reflective of our underlying anxieties and fears about not feeling safe or secure in the world. When we knot our muscles, clench our teeth, or tie our guts in knots, it does little for us but cause pain, raise blood pressure, and create more noise in the nervous system. While this bracing accomplishes the unconscious task of dulling our sensitivity and shielding us from the intensity of life, it also exhausts, depletes, and weakens us. Such survival skills are not sustainable and, over time, the accumulating stress and strain will lead to many problems.

Relaxation is a means of ceasing to create pain for ourselves. Often the first strategy we teach people to relax is to actually increase the level of their tension! Why? Because when we realize that we can increase the tension—say, take it from a "4" up to a "7"—we recognize that we really are in control of, or at least can influence, the situation and our response to it. No one can make us tense, no matter how much blame we may want to project onto others. If we can *increase* our tension, then it is also possible for us to *release* it, to relax from a "7" back down to a "4," and with practice down to a "3," "2," or even "zero." As we gradually learn to recognize and reduce the habits that create noise in our bodies and minds, we learn to relax and open our bodies, minds, hearts, and souls to commune with creation in all its many dimensions.

Dynamic relaxation—the state of optimal tension, free from unnecessary strain—is a gesture of mercy and compassion toward ourselves. To make this step again and again takes courage—the courage to look, listen, feel, and welcome life without running away, or constricting back into our shell of tension, or *ignore*-ance. At the sacred heart of the Islamic faith, the first words of worship are *Bismillah Erachman, Erahim:* "We begin in the name of Allah, the One who is Merciful and Compassionate." Taking this prayer to heart, we come to realize that this is where our work on ourselves must begin: to begin to open our hearts with greater mercy and compassion toward ourselves and others.

THOUGHTS TO ENERGIZE YOUR MEDITATION

Consider the precious opportunity that this human existence gives us. By practicing meditation we can realize and express our enormous potential. This is a great gift.

Then consider impermanence. Whatever is born will die, whatever appears will disappear. Recognizing this, we understand that we really don't know how much time we have to realize our true nature and potential and to love and help those we care for.

Contemplating the laws of cause and effect, we understand that we have choice in our lives. What we experience today is largely the result of the choices we made previously, and what we choose to do, think, and say now will shape and determine our future.

Finally, consider why we should work with our minds. The long-term result, the experience of enlightenment, is more joyful, intense, and complete than anything we have yet known, and once found can never be lost. Secondly, there is so much suffering in the world, and our ability to benefit others is very limited if we ourselves are confused.

So, for ourselves and others, we want to place our trust in those who can inspire and guide us in this inner work and in the traditions, teachings, and methods that help us to master our minds and to awaken genuine wisdom and compassion in our lives.

FAITH, SUPPORT, AND INSPIRATION

For all these reasons, then, we seek a refuge from the chaos and confusion within and around us. Like a child taking refuge in its mother, or hikers seeking shelter from a storm, we seek an oasis of sanity in a chaotic world.

Outwardly, we place our trust in the teachers who remind us through their example, their kindness, and their teachings that it is possible to become free from mental and emotional confusion and to become wise and kind as well. We find strength and guidance in the teachings that show us how to master our minds and find freedom and understanding in our lives. Likewise, we find refuge in the community of friends and companions who share our study, practice, and investigation of how meditation can be practically applied to meet the challenges and opportunities of daily life.

Inwardly, the teacher reflects the seed of our own potential for deep understanding and genuine kindness. Oral and written teachings point our minds toward the ineffable wisdom that shines like the sun and moves within our hearts, the real mystery that precedes life and endures beyond death. Our companions along the way remind us of the community of people who, from the beginning of time, strove to find the same understanding and who preserved and passed on the teachings.

Meditation—whether you are sitting alone in a cave, or in an office, or meditating in a group—does not happen in a vacuum, devoid of relationship and sharing with others. Affirming, trusting, and drawing strength and inspiration from your relationships with others and your connectedness with the universe will offer you protection and peace of mind, and will inspire your meditation practice.

PROPER MOTIVATION

As you begin each session, remind yourself of why you are sitting down to meditate. Why are you giving yourself this gift of time for centering, harmonizing, and fine-tuning? To avoid pain? To be happy? To find peace? To rest or energize?

Remember, as you grow in clarity and peace of mind you directly contribute to bringing peace and understanding to others. And as you develop patience toward the people and situations that previously triggered frustration, you will be filling the universe with compassion instead of anger, understanding instead of confusion.

Our intentions reflect back to us an echo of the same energy. How often have you seen actions motivated by fear emphasize the paranoia of a situation? And how often have your love and care touched and opened the heart of another?

Remember, it is not what you do but how and why you do it that really matters. You always have a choice, so use it wisely, compassionately, and creatively.

MONITOR YOUR MEDITATION

Your meditation session is likely to go through several phases. Once you have settled down you should stabilize your attention by practicing a concentration technique for a few moments. Then you can apply your mind to whatever meditation—mindfulness, reflective, creative, or heart-centered—you choose. Throughout the session, use your vigilance or introspective alertness to monitor the quality of the focus of your attention. In this way you can recognize when your attention has wandered off or faded away. If you find it difficult to stay with the meditation because of too much distraction or dullness, you will find it useful to balance your mind again with a few minutes of concentration meditation, especially by watching the breath. Then, once again, return to your main meditation.

DEDICATION AND SHARING

Take a few moments at the end of each session to consciously extend and share the positive energies you have accumulated. From your heart radiate out into space warmth, light, and love, and imagine it touching others as a vibration that calms, energizes, heals, comforts, and nourishes. Be creative! Imagine you are playing a mental video game. Beam all your positive feelings to your friends, family, people you feel neutral toward, even to your enemies. Realize that they all, just like you, want to be happy, want to escape suffering and pain, and desire to make the most of their lives. Imagine radiating all the positive energy you have generated through your meditation out to all beings, and that each receives from you whatever they most need at that moment to carry them from fragmentation toward wholeness. In this way, realize that this inner work on yourself is also an offering to the world. (See the Dedication Meditation beginning on page 243 for a more detailed explanation.)

CARRY-OVER PRACTICE

Through your practice of meditation, it is possible to develop many previously latent positive qualities. Having used the brief period of your quiet meditation to touch and develop the peace, clarity, understanding, kindness, and vitality within, you now face the challenge of carrying these qualities into dynamic action as you move through the world. Throughout the day, consciously recall and reenergize these feelings. Particularly when you start to rush and tumble, internally pause, center, and move toward the sense of harmony you experienced earlier in meditation. Periods of quiet, undistracted meditation are precious opportunities to get in touch with qualities that will gradually grow and pervade even your busiest activities.

You will find that any activity can become an opportunity to train your mind, develop concentration, refine your awareness, deepen your insight, practice patience or loving-kindness. Live in a creative and meditative way, as though your life were a dream and you are busy waking up.

REMEMBER THE INNER SMILE

Lest you get too serious, it's important to approach your meditations with a sense of curiosity and playful inquisitiveness. For many people, holding a gentle inner smile during meditation helps to prevent them from trying too hard, getting tense, or being too self-critical. Enjoy your practice! Smile! Be playful!

FIVE STEPS FOR
A DAILY MEDITATION PRACTICE

In establishing a daily meditation practice, the following guidelines can help add variety and richness. Your confidence in weaving these pieces together will grow with practice and this simple flow will become quite natural. There are five parts to this sequence:

1. Inspriation and Intention: As you begin, take a short time to clarify your intention and offer a prayer of gratitude or a call for inspiration. Remember that meditation is the practice of deep relationships, and that you never practice "alone." Call upon the sources of inspiration in your life, that they may inspire your meditation. Remembering all those who share your life and world, practice in order to in some way be a force of healing and wholeness in the world.

2. Concentration: Next, shift to some type of focusing, concentration meditation, such as mindfulness of breathing, the nine-part breath, or the elemental breaths.

3. Meditation: Now shift to a longer period of quiet meditation using whatever technique you are drawn to.

4. Dedication: Finally, end the session with a brief dedication, gathering the potency generated through this time of meditation into your heart and radiating it to share the blessings with all beings.

5. Application: As you conclude your formal meditation practice, make a smooth transition and hold

the intention to carry the quality of mindful presence into whatever activities will follow. Throughout the day, pause from time to time for a mini-meditation to renew your connection to these qualities, and then continue to infuse your life with the mindful presence, insight, creativity, and compassion that flow from your meditation practice.

Though these five stages build upon each other, if time or inclination do not permit, you will still benefit from doing only steps 1, 2, and 4, steps 1 and 2, or even just step 1. Give yourself credit for any sincere steps that you make in the right direction!

Keep your formal practice short and simple at first so that you can begin to establish this new life-habit and feel some success in maintaining it. Then, as you see the benefits, gradually develop, deepen, or expand your practice.

TAKING REFUGE: RECEIVING AND RADIATING SPIRITUAL STRENGTH

There is one meditation that is universally useful as a preliminary practice for all other meditations. Because it is so fundamentally important, we would like to offer it here, to serve as a bridge to the rest of the meditations that follow. Technically, it would be classified as belonging to the "creative" category of meditation, and although it often serves as a foundation for other meditations to build on, it is also a complete and potent practice on its own.

This training is based on a profound principle found universally in the contemplative traditions, sometimes described as "taking refuge." One of the most beautiful references for it is found in the Holy Koran, and is expressed in this exquisite translation by Sufi Sheik Lex Hixon:

> With each breath may we take refuge in the Living Truth alone, released from coarse arrogance and subtle pride. May every thought and action be intended in the Supremely Holy Name, Allah, as a direct expression of boundless Divine Compassion and Most Tender Love. May the exaltation of endless praise arising spontaneously as the life of endless beings flow consciously toward the Single Source of Being, Source of the intricate evolution of endless worlds. May we be guided through every experience along the Direct Path of Love that leads from the Human Heart into the Most Sublime Source of Love.

A survey of the world's spiritual traditions reveals a common grounding in a trinity of refuges that support meditation practice:

- ๑ First, we take refuge in the living examples of great teachers who have kept the tradition alive and guided others in its ways.

- ๑ Second, we take refuge in the inspiring body of spiritual teachings that offer practical principles, techniques, and advice on how to live a truly righteous and balanced life.

- ๑ Third, we take refuge in fellowship with the spiritual community of kindred souls who walk the path with us, and who are a source of companionship and support along the way.

Each of these factors provides the nourishment and support essential to meditation practice. Bombarded by the intensity and complexity of our life, it is easy to feel overwhelmed: "How can I possibly manage this situation?" We all need help, guidance, and inspiration to find our way and to stay the course at times when we may become distracted or disheartened. Incorporating the practice of taking refuge into the beginning of a meditation session offers a sense of deep connection and groundedness that supercharges your practice with inspiration and strength greater than your small, limited self. Here is one way to awaken the mind of refuge in your meditations:

As you sit here now, envision yourself sitting at the center of your universe, surrounded by all living beings. Holding this image in mind, pause for a moment to remember, invite, or sense the presence of those who have most deeply inspired you in your life. Reach out now from your heart, and with your hands, to these beings whose presence in your life is truly a blessing, a source of renewal, deep information, and inspiration. Imagine that all of them are right here with you now, surrounding you and shining like a constellation of brilliant suns. Or, if you like, envision that these many sources of light merge into a single brighter sun that shines a radiance of blessings and inspiration into your life.

Imagine that with each breath you reach out to them and hold their hands, and that through your connection with them you can draw strength and inspiration. In fact, the stronger and more sincere your own aspiration, the deeper and stronger the flow of inspiration becomes. Imagine that each of these inspiring people in turn reaches out to hold the hands of those to whom they look for guidance, strength, and inspiration, and that they in turn reach out to those who have inspired them. Sense your teachers reaching out to their teachers, who reach out to their teachers.... Envision yourself balanced within and receiving from this endless cascade of wisdom and love as it flows to you and through you from countless inspired ancestors of the far and distant past.

Envision this inspiration as knowledge and energy soaking into you now. It energizes the parts where your life-force is weak. It balances what needs to be balanced. It floods, cleanses, and opens the spaces and places within you that are clogged or congested, and nourishes the seeds of your deepest potential to blossom beautifully. Like sunlight filtering into a deep, clear pool, sense these waves of inspiring grace flooding your mindbody-energy-spirit. Every dimension of your being is illuminated, blessed, and renewed. With each breath you are filled, saying silently "receiving." With each breath you release what you no longer need to hold on to, saying inwardly "releasing." Receiving . . . releasing . . . receiving . . . releasing. . . . Plugging into this renewal circuit, you are revitalized, calmed, and energized, and move toward balance between your inner and outer worlds.

Having cleared your circuits, charged your batteries, and filled your tanks, begin now to radiate and expand this sense of peace and well-being within you. With each inhalation, shift to receive, and then with each exhalation, radiate. Breathing in, imagine the inspiration and blessings converging and spiraling into you, filling your heart. With each out-breath, sense, imagine, or feel your heart silently radiating like a bright, shining star. Effortlessly offer the natural radiance of your innermost being to the world. Allow it to shine through the darkness within or around you. Allow it to light up your inner and outer world effortlessly, immediately. Let this be the light of your love, the light of your peace, the light of your presence, the light of your goodwill and positive regard.

Now, having enhanced and expanded your radiance, begin to direct your attention and energy to the world around you. Reach out to those who look to you as a source of inspiration, guidance, and support. Reach out to your children, your students, your patients, your clients and customers, and to all those who look to you as they seek balance and belonging in their lives. Receiving inspiration, wisdom, and strength from those you draw guidance from, reach out with your hands and from your heart and let each exhalation become an inspiring gift that you offer to those who, in turn, look to you.

Envision each person you reach out to taking your gift to heart, and feel that it truly inspires and awakens greater wisdom, balance, and strength in their lives. As you reach out to your children, envision them receiving and taking this gift to heart and then passing it on to their children, who pass it on to their children, who pass it on to their children, and to all whose lives they touch. Envision your students reaching out to their students who reach out to their students. Imagine that all those to whom you reach out take these gifts to heart and pass them on to those who will pass them on, in an endless cascade of inspiration and blessings that reaches out into the world to help awaken all beings to their True Nature, nurturing harmony and wholeness for countless generations to come.

In this way, receiving and radiating, sense yourself balanced here, reaching out from this fleeting moment where all the experiences of the infinite past and all the potential for the boundless future converge. Viewed in this light, realize that your real life-work is to reach out and realize your connectedness and wholeness, to deepen in balance, to increase your capacity to gather inspiration and wisdom, to take it to heart and pass it on as far and wide as you possibly can. From the depths of your being, generate a deep and heartfelt aspiration to awaken fully to your True Nature and potential and to help all beings do the same, so that they in turn can inspire others to awaken fully.

Imagine the silent light of your innermost being blazing with exquisite clarity and radiating out to fill your body. Imagine it radiating out into the world around you now, and sense yourself as a lighthouse of love, a radiant source of inspiration for all beings. Holding your loved ones and friends in mind, radiate this love to them. Bring to heart and mind the leaders of the world, the children of the world, the beleaguered nations and species of the world, and radiate your heartfelt care and prayers to them.

In this way, receiving . . . radiating, each breath affirms your deep relationship with the whole of creation, and with all beings in the past, present, and future. In this way, each blessed breath becomes a gesture of balance, a gesture of receiving from and offering to all.

Sense, imagine, and affirm that those you offer to are actually helped and inspired by the love and energy you radiate to them. Envision their tensions, worry, or fear melting away. They are inspired, renewed, and moved toward harmony and balance through your influence. Out of gratitude they radiate back to you waves of thanksgiving and blessings. These add to the waves of your inspiration. You radiate and offer your heartfelt thanks to those who inspire you, and they in turn, pleased and inspired by your gratitude and generosity, then radiate even more energy, inspiration, and blessings to you. This reciprocal and responsive flow radiates in both directions like a figure eight of receiving and radiating. As this flow circulates, it seems that everyone in the loop receives exactly what they need to find harmony and balance and to awaken to their own True Nature and potential in their lives in this moment.

Rest in this flow for as long as you like. Then either shift into another meditation, using the sense of refuge and deep connectedness as a springboard and foundation, or make a gentle transition into whatever activity comes next. As you refocus your attention into other matters, simply allow this sense of deep relatedness to remain active as it slips more into the background of your awareness. Throughout the day remember that this deep connectedness and flow is only a thought or a breath away. Now and then, as you are involved with other things, with a natural mindful breath reach out and take refuge in this deep connectedness as you continue to receive and radiate. When in doubt, remember these four things: "reach out," "plug in," "receive," and "radiate."

Practiced in this way, taking refuge and receiving and radiating is a complete meditation practice in itself. It is also a wonderful preliminary meditation that can be done for a few minutes prior to any other practice to infuse it with many blessings. Take some time to let this expanded sense of yourself and your relatedness integrate. Notice how finding yourself in this circle of wholeness changes, expands, and impacts your sense of yourself, your sense of connectedness, your sense of balance, and your sense of being.

The seeker who sets out upon the Way
Shines bright over the world.
But day and night the person who is awake
Shines in the radiance of the spirit.
Meditate.
Live purely.
Be quiet.
Do your work, with mastery.
Like the moon, come out from behind the clouds!
Shine.

—Shakyamuni Buddha

THREE
CONCENTRATION MEDITATION

*Concentration is like a diamond, a brilliant
focusing of our energy, intelligence, and sensitivity.*

FOCUSING THE MIND

We have all, at different times in our lives, had a taste of concentration: each of us has fully given our attention to a loved one, a beautiful sunset, a resounding symphony, or a project that completely absorbed us. And it is possible to train our minds to increase and develop this special kind of focused attention.

By developing our ability to concentrate, we increase our capacity for integrating thoughts, fact, and information in a way that reveals deeper, more integral wisdom than that which is immediately apparent to the unfocused observer. The concentrated mind enables us to accelerate our growth and learning because it provides more intuitive insight into the true nature and meaning of life.

Life is learning. The amount of real learning that takes place is directly proportional to our ability to concentrate or focus our attention on a chosen object or theme for a period of time. Real learning is not just the acquisition of knowledge but the ability to penetrate deeply into the meaning behind superficial knowledge and appearances.

For most people, the distracted and uncontrolled circulation of thoughts is the norm. Yet such confused states of mind are problematic and do little to improve the quality of our lives. The father of modern psychology of consciousness, Dr. William James, once said that the maximum attention span of a normal person was four seconds. For most of us, even that would be a feat! While this is regarded as normal by modern standards, the world's contemplative traditions regard this as highly dysfunctional compared to what is really possible if people were to develop their potential. The archives of the great contemplative traditions yield a treasury of inspiring descriptions of, and systematic directions for, developing states of concentration that remain stable and clear for minutes, hours, even days at a time without distraction!

CONCENTRATION, CONTEMPLATION, AND UNIFICATION

Developing strong concentration is similar to developing physical strength. With patient, persistent practice, the following techniques will increase the strength and duration of your attention. Once this capacity is developed, a concentrated beam of awareness can be focused on any activity, leading to deeper understanding and appreciation of the ways things truly are and greater wisdom and compassion in your life.

Classic spiritual literature describes several stages of concentrative meditation, each with clear indicators. A simple way to understand these stages follows:

At the first stage, concentration is momentary, then gradually sustained. A classical indicator that our practice of concentration is becoming more stable is when we can focus our attention on a chosen object or theme for seven, then twenty-one, then 108 breaths without losing focus. As concentration grows, even when our attention does wander, distractions are immediately recognized and we return our mind to the object of concentration.

At the second stage, concentration is so stable that we no longer completely lose focus. As we develop our capacity to sustain our focus of attention without lapsing into distraction or dullness, concentration ripens and matures into a state of contemplation or communion with whatever we are focused on. Here we begin to experience a profound sense of connectedness and flow between ourselves as the observer and the object of our contemplation.

Finally, at the third stage, concentration and the sense of communion become so wholehearted and uninterrupted that the mind literally absorbs the object of its focus and merges into a state of unification. You may have spontaneously experienced such complete concentration at times—when you were in love, for example, or when your attention was completely captured by something of inspiring beauty. In such timeless moments we transcend the duality of "connection" and enter a state of ecstasy in which the subject (self) becomes intimately unified with the object in a state of profound intuitive understanding. As the great Tibetan saint Tilopa once said, "At first the meditator feels like his mind is tumbling like a river falling through a gorge; in mid-course, it flows slowly like the gently meandering River Ganges; and finally, the river becomes one with the great vast Ocean, where the Lights of Son (self) and Mother (ground of being) merge into one."

As our concentration grows more stable, our perception and conception of ourselves and our world gradually transform and new dimensions of intuitive insight are revealed. Our sense of separation and isolation gives way to a heartfelt sense of connection, intimacy, interrelatedness, belonging, empathy, respect, love and compassion—for ourselves, for other "selves," and for the world and universe in which we live. Most important, through the practice of concentration meditation we awaken the profound insight necessary to transform our perception of the world; we realize that a world of separate objects and entities is truly a compelling, though widely shared illusion, an artifact of the distracted mind. The journey from distraction to concentration, communion, and unification is truly one that leads us toward discovering the many dimensions of our wholeness.

MOTIVATIONS

In the classic meditation manuals, meditative concentration or *samadhi* (Sanskrit), is developed through cultivating a state of mental stabilization known as "calm abiding"— *shamatha* (Sanskrit) or *shine* (Tibetan). These progressive stages of deep meditation open the doorways to various levels of meditative absorption or trance known as the *dhyanas* (Sanskrit). The meditative practices for developing concentration have traditionally been cultivated with the motivation to achieve one or more of the following results:

⊚ The most common motivation is to develop greater calm and clarity of mind and to reduce the ignorance, confusion, and suffering caused by mental agitation and dullness.

ꙅ Classically, concentrative meditation is regarded as the precursor to all the other meditations that appear later in this section. Through mastery of concentration, the mind develops the coherence it needs to become a reliable instrument for investigating and understanding the deep, multidimensional nature of reality Once developed, the concentrated mind is then applied to enhancing the effectiveness of mindfulness meditations, reflective meditations, and creative meditations in order to supercharge those practices with the focused power of presence necessary to penetrate the illusions of habitual perceptions and conceptions, and reveal the true nature of reality to us directly.

ꙅ A third motivation for developing concentrative power is to generate a state of bliss. This, unfortunately, can be quite seductive and lead to a false sense of having achieved an advanced state of spiritual evolution. Becoming attached to the blissfulness that arises from concentration meditation is a sure way to arrest your meditative and spiritual evolution.

ꙅ A fourth motivation is the wish to develop a broad spectrum of psychic powers. When fully developed and correctly applied, concentration gives rise to a dazzling array of extraordinary human capacities, including clairvoyance, telepathy, and mind-travel. Many of the classic meditation texts provide detailed step-by-step instructions on how to awaken these abilities once sufficient powers of concentration have been developed. Yet again, due to the seductive, blissful, intensity of these practices and the dangers of abusing these powers, meditators are traditionally warned to avoid pursuing this path of development unless they have first developed the ethical maturity necessary to approach these practices with a genuinely altruistic motivation that is free from self-centered personal desires. To pursue this path without a strong moral foundation and the wisdom to direct these powers is regarded as extremely dangerous.

In modern times such extraordinary, though natural, powers of the mind are regarded as rare, or even mythical. This is due to the ignorance of those who lack faith and who have never had the inclination and discipline necessary to engage in the intensive meditation practice with which they are cultivated. Out of their wisdom and compassion for others, those who have cultivated these powers are likely to avoid debates with people who flaunt their ignorance, and simply go about their lives with a gentle smile of deep compassion and understanding.

CONCENTRATION IS A BALANCING ACT

Training in concentration performs a miracle of transformation. When we have the kind of stability of mind common in sleep, we lack the clarity necessary for the mind to be a truly useful instrument. On the other hand, during wakeful life the clarity of our minds may be very vivid, such as when we are interested, aroused, threatened, angry, or delighted. At these times, however, we are often also mentally agitated and lacking in the steadiness of attention necessary to carefully examine what is going on and to respond in a wise, compassionate, and effective manner.

The challenge for the meditator is to develop the rare and delicate balance in the nervous system necessary for sustained awareness. Some liken concentration meditation to learning how to balance on the top of a mountain with two very steep slopes on either side. One side is the turbulent valley of agitation, the mind boiling over with excitement which, if taken to extremes, is called psychosis. On the other side is the danger of sinking into the valley of mental dullness where awareness fades, and sleepiness renders us unconscious to our life and world.

To keep the mind balanced in concentration, you must learn to cultivate two qualities of mind: first, the stability and continuity of attention that can remain focused upon whatever you choose, inwardly or outwardly. Second, along with that stability is a quality of lucid clarity and presence that illuminates whatever you focus upon. This unusually balanced mental state is a rare fusion of high intensity with deep peace and stability of mind. Free from the disturbing habits of distraction and mental dullness, the concentrated mind is able to focus deeply into whatever it holds. This reveals a quality of extraordinary intuitive insight that frees us from the confusion generated by the habits of a dull and wild mind.

MINDFULNESS AND VIGILANCE

Two qualities of mind are regarded as necessary to develop the stability and vividness necessary for sustained concentration. The first is called mindfulness. Mindful awareness is the faculty of attention that is able to focus without distraction, without forgetfulness, and with continuity of awareness upon whatever you choose to attend to. The Sanskrit and Arabic terms for mindfulness are often translated as "remembering" or "recollection." In Hebrew, mindfulness carries the meaning of "deep listening" or "giving your heart to something." To the degree that mindfulness is strong, we are able to maintain awareness of whatever we choose without lapsing into distraction or forgetting what we were paying attention to.

Though in recent years the practice of mindfulness has received considerable attention, mindfulness alone is not sufficient to perfect concentration. Mindfulness must work in tandem with a second quality of mind—vigilance or discernment. Sometimes also described as "introspective alertness," this quality of mind serves as a metacognition that monitors our quality of mindfulness. Such an inner "quality control" function keeps us aware of the status of our mental balance, alerting us if the mind is congealing into dullness or churning with too much excitement. In practice, vigilance is like a mother who checks in frequently on her sleeping child. She isn't there constantly but checks in from time to time: "How is the baby? Is everything alright?" In the same way, vigilance checks to see if our attention is present or has gone out to lunch, or if our attention has forgotten our chosen focus and wandered off into memories of the past or fantasies of the future. If vigilance detects that either agitation or dullness are creeping into the mind and threatening mindfulness, it activates our will to apply antidotes to restore our balance of mind.

CONCENTRATION AND INTIMACY

Concentration meditation increases our capacity not only for living life with a greater intensity but also with greater capacity for intimacy. For many people, when the intimacy or intensity of life reaches a threshold that exceeds their capacity to hold it, they become frightened and withdraw. To escape the intensity of really feeling close or intimate with others, people usually either seek a way to dull their sensitivity or to release the charge of intensity building within them. Strategies for reducing sensitivity include: dulling ourselves with nicotine, alcohol, or over-eating; dampening our physical sensitivity by carrying excess tension or extra weight; or keeping ourselves busy, agitated, and distracted. Sometimes, as a subtle way to reduce the charge of intensity that is building within us, we breathe through our mouth instead of our nose. Strategies commonly used to release intensity are to be fidgety—tapping our fingers or feet, talking too much, nervously cracking jokes, or seeking intense emotional or sexual release.

The practices of concentration and mindfulness meditation strengthen the clarity and peace of mind necessary to be truly present, which gives rise to a sense of intimacy with ourselves and with others. Concentration helps us not only to increase our capacity for connection and intimacy, but to live in a more centered, patient, tolerant, thoughtful, and compassionate way.

SELECTING A FOCUS FOR CONCENTRATION

The first step in concentration meditation is to select a focus for concentration. There are thousands of objects of attention that are classically prescribed for developing concentration. An ideal concentration focus for you will be one that is sufficiently easy for your attention to find and hold with clarity, and one that brings peace or joy to your mind but doesn't create too much excitement or boredom as you focus on it. If you select a focus that has meaning for you, be watchful that it doesn't create too many associations or distractions.

For most people, the simplest and most direct method for developing mental stability and concentration is to focus upon the flow of your breath—the steady balancing rhythm of in-breath and out-breath. The breath is often used because it is easy to find and continually present—we breathe approximately 21,600 times every day. Meditating on the flow of breath is considered the most effective method for helping people with busy minds to quiet their internal dialogue. Our state of mind and flow of breath are very closely connected. You can observe for yourself how closely linked breathing patterns and states of mind are. Notice the changes in your own rate and flow of breath when you are feeling anxious, angry, joyful, loving, stressed, or at peace. Simply by bringing your attention to the natural rhythm and flow of your breath you can shift your mind and body toward greater calm, clarity, and balance.

If you select the breath as a focus for concentration meditation, simply focus either upon the sensations as the breath flows in and out of the nostrils, or upon the sensations of the abdomen rising and falling with each breath.

Even if you choose another focus for training your concentration, it can still be helpful to begin with a few minutes of mindful breathing to help focus and quiet your mind. Allow each inhalation to help you focus, and each exhalation to help you let your attention flow toward whatever you are focused upon. Focus . . . flow . . . focus . . . flow . . .

Since the breath is your constant companion, it can help you carry concentration meditation over into the rest of your life. Each breath can help you focus and flow, and establish calm intensity, harmony, and balanced presence in the moment. Each breath, if taken to heart, can also offer profound insights about cycles of change and impermanence, about receiving and releasing, and can affirm your intimate connection and belonging to the whole of creation.

If you are physically oriented, you might find that holding a certain posture or doing some simple repetitive movements may help you focus your concentration. A meditative gesture or *mudra* held in stillness or repeated again and again, a yoga posture, or a rhythmic exercise such as jogging or cycling can also help you begin to develop the initial stages of concentration if you use it as a focal point for wholehearted attention.

You might also choose an outer object of the senses, such as a sacred symbol or object, a picture, or an object of beauty as a focus for concentration. Some traditions recommend focusing on the elements of earth, fire, water, air, or space; others emphasize focusing upon various centers within the body, such as the "heart chakra" at the center of the chest or the *hara* or *tantien* point a few inches below the navel.

If you have a devotional orientation, an object of special symbolic significance can serve well in the development of one-pointed concentration. Choose a picture of a special source of inspiration in your life or a sacred symbol or object. Some traditions use the repetition of a short prayer, a line of scripture, or a mantra, while others focus on the contemplation of the names of God or of Divine attributes, such as mercy, compassion, patience, strength, beauty, or limitlessness, to develop concentration. Choosing a devotional object for your meditation may offer an inspiring wholehearted focus that touches your heart and uplifts your spirit.

Some people focus their concentration meditation on a visualized object within the inner space of the mind. In this case, the meditator calls forth the image in his or her mind, and then generates the mindfulness and vigilance necessary to first develop stable awareness of the mental object, then to develop a clear image of the object. Classic mental images used to develop concentration in this way include sacred symbols such as an image of the Buddha or Christ, a Cross, Star of David, or Kabbalistic Tree of Life; a mandala or medicine wheel; a blue flower or simply the color blue; or the mental image of a luminous self-sounding sacred word or syllable, such as Ah or Om, Allah, or Shalom.

Subtler "objects" of concentration may include a mental quality or theme, such as boundless love, joy, compassion, peace, or the formless luminous presence of mind. Focal points such as these are generally considered so subtle and difficult to hold in mind that a novice meditator would have more difficulty developing concentration if relying on them.

At one level, the selected focus for attention may hold a potent symbolic significance that imprints the mind through its contemplation. At another level, the actual nature of the object is considered less significant since it serves a somewhat instrumental value as a "strange attractor" to anchor and organize our attention. We once heard a revered meditation teacher say that you could use a box of tissue paper as a focal point to develop concentration, because it was the training of the mind, not the object, that was most important!

BALANCE IS THE KEY TO
DEVELOPING CONCENTRATION

Once you start to learn to concentrate, you will find that your mind will sway between holding its object too tightly or too loosely. It is important to find the balance between these two. Once you have settled your mind on your object and are focusing your attention, relax your mind a little. If you grasp too tightly at your object, your mind will become agitated and your body tense. If you relax too much, however, your attention will wander or fade.

With practice and patience, you will learn to distinguish between these two states and find the balance necessary to deepen your concentration.

CLARITY AND STABILITY

As you begin your practice of concentration meditation, it is best to first give emphasis to cultivating the stability of your attention toward your chosen image/object. If you make efforts to increase the clarity or vividness of your focus at the beginning, you will create more turbulence in the mind-stream and disturb the subtle balance of the nervous system. If this happens, you may practice for years with only frustration to show for it. Drawing on millennia of insight and advice from contemplative scientists who have refined these inner arts, focus first on developing a stable continuity of attention, and then gradually begin to enhance the vivid clarity of your object.

At first this can seem like trying to focus on an island shrouded in fog: you know it's out there, and you just keep your mind intent and focused in that direction even though it doesn't appear at all clearly to you. Gradually, with practice, your attention will grow more stable and the flow of your attention will melt through the fog, allowing the vividness and clarity of the object to increase.

When you first begin to practice concentration meditation, you'll probably only be able to hold the object of focus in your mind for a couple of seconds before distraction or dullness set in. Be patient; don't get discouraged. In the beginning, the habits of distraction and dullness will be much stronger than the newly emerging habit of concentration. As you continue to cultivate mindfulness with vigilance, the continuity of your awareness will grow until you are able to stay focused with less distraction. When your concentration becomes more stable and you are able to stay focused without losing the awareness of your object for a longer period, you can then begin to increase the clarity of the mind.

ANTIDOTES TO EXCESSIVE MENTAL ENERGY

To reduce mental agitation and develop greater peace and stability of mind, a number of strategies can help. For instance, reflective meditation on a theme that will sober your mind can help to dampen the "roller-coaster" of hyperactivity and turbulence. Common themes for this type of reflection are contemplating the nature of change and impermanence, the sufferings of humanity, the inevitability of death, and the precious opportunities of your life. If you are distracted by strong compulsive desires for something or someone, contemplate the scenario through in its entirety, focusing on the full life-cycle of the object or person you desire. Vividly imagine yourself getting what you crave, and then play the story out in your mind. Seeing what you are ultimately left with can help calm the excitement of such unsatisfied desire. Contemplate these themes with compassion; when mental excitation has settled down, immediately return your attention back to the focus of your concentration.

ANTIDOTES TO MENTAL DULLNESS

When the mind is dull and you want to boost the level of your mental clarity, a number of physical adjustments can be helpful. Experiment with sitting with your spine very straight, turning up the lights in the room, or raising your gaze. To refresh your mind try going for a mindful walk, taking a brisk shower or splashing cold water in your face, or looking up at the sky. One teacher suggested that if we were sleepy during meditation, we might imagine that we were sitting on top of a telephone pole, or even go and sit on the edge of a cliff to increase the likelihood that we would stay wakeful!

Here are some mental strategies you can use as an antidote to dullness and to uplift mental energy:

- ☙ Visualize filling your body with light.
- ☙ Imagine the mind as being of the nature of light.
- ☙ Visualize your mind as a sphere of radiant white light at your heart and imagine it rising up through the crown of your head to merge into the vastness of space.
- ☙ Reflect on things that cheer you up, lighten your mood, or expand and open your heart and mind.
- ☙ Contemplate the inspiring example of people you admire, the benefits of kindness, the qualities of someone you really love, or other things or people in your life for which you are grateful.

If you are really getting stuck or having a difficult time, end your meditation session. If you are tired, relax, take a nap, or soak in the tub. If you are agitated, go for a mindful walk, jog, or put on some mellow music that you enjoy dancing to. See how compassionately creative you can be in redirecting the unproductive energy of your mind.

FOCUSING AND QUIETING THE MIND

Sit comfortably and take a few minutes to relax. Rest your hands in your lap and quietly and gently smile to yourself. Bring your attention to your breath and feel the sensation of the air flowing out of your nostrils. Now, start to count each exhalation, from one to ten. If you lose count, return to one. If you are unable to reach ten, start again at one.

You can use this technique at any time during the day, even for a few minutes. The aim is to bring your attention to a keen yet relaxed focus on what you are doing. Don't try too hard to concentrate; allow your mind to be alert and relaxed. Inevitably your mind will wander, but whenever it does simply return to the next breath. As Saint Francis de Sales once said, "If the heart wanders or is distracted, bring it back to the point quite gently . . . and even if you did nothing during the whole of your hour (of contemplation) but bring your heart back, though it went away every time you bring it back, your hour would be very well employed." With practice your concentration will grow stronger and you will find it easier to keep your mind on whatever you are doing.

AN ANTIDOTE TO DISCOURAGEMENT

It is easy to feel that your meditation session has been a waste of time if much of it is taken up with distraction or agitation. A simple remedy to this, and another way to develop concentration, is to break up your hour-long or half-hour session into many smaller sessions with very short breaks in between. (You can also use this method any time you have a few moments to spare.)

1. Sit comfortably with the spine straight.

2. Gently and completely exhale.

3. As you exhale, softly vocalize the sound "ahhh." Allow the sound to open and flow outward. Allow your mind to open and flow with the sound as one continuous wave of awareness, until it reaches the moment when distraction or agitation arises.

4. At the first sign of distraction or agitation, immediately stop the session.

5. Relax. Take a break for fifteen to twenty seconds. Look around, stretch your legs if you like, then repeat steps 2 to 5.

Repeat these steps as many times as you like within the time you have allowed for your session. Gradually you will become accustomed to these short spans of continuous attention and applied concentration. Initially your concentration will last for only a few seconds, but with practice you will develop stability and the depth and duration of your concentration will grow.

As your concentration develops, consciously feel that your mind and the sound of "ahhh" are continuously opening outward, even when you stop the "ahhh" to take another breath.

ZEN BREATHING EXERCISE

As concentration and attention increase, the mind becomes clear and balanced. More and more sharply we see how things are changing in each instant, how these are ultimately not a source of lasting happiness, and how the whole mind-body process flows according to certain laws empty of any permanent self. . . .
These profound insights become clear simply from increasing mindfulness, penetrating awareness of our own process. With these insights wisdom arises, bringing equanimity, loving-kindness, and compassion, for in experiencing the emptiness of self we see the unity of all things.

—Jack Kornfield

Sit comfortably with your spine straight. Establish a proper motivation for beginning the session, and start with a gentle smile in mind. Bring your attention either to the sensation of the flow of breath at the tip of your nostrils, or to your abdomen as you inhale and exhale naturally. Consciously take a few deep breaths, but do not strain. Simply emphasize the movement in order to clarify the sensations you are attending to. Now, allow the flow of breath to find its own natural rhythm. Allow the body to breathe without interference. Allow the inhalations and exhalations to come and go, effortlessly keeping a keen awareness of the process. Gently and unwaveringly allow your attention to float on the changing rhythms of your in- and out-breath. Whenever your attention wanders or becomes diffused— and it quite often will—gently but firmly bring your awareness back to the breath. The aim is not to arrive anywhere but to develop the capacity to be fully present each moment, one after another.

Don't be discouraged or disheartened by distractions or mental dullness. This is to be expected. With practice, you will be able to catch the distractions and bring your attention back to your breath. Eventually your concentration will stabilize and even though distraction will still arise you will be able to stay unwaveringly upon your object of concentration. You will have developed the capacity to bring a continuum of undistracted, deeply penetrating attention to whatever field of perception or contemplation you choose.

The force of the mind and its illuminating, penetrating capacity, once developed, is similar to the power and coherence of a laser beam, compared to the flickering candlelight of our ordinary distracted states of consciousness. The power and clarity of a finely-tuned mind is one of the most useful tools that a human being can develop.

BREATHING EASY

Sit comfortably and relax, and bring your awareness to your breathing. As you breathe out, naturally dissolve and let go of all the negative energy you wish to be free from. As you breathe in, allow the breath to naturally and effortlessly fill you with the positive qualities you want to be energized by. Allow the breath to fill you as a natural reflex to the deep exhalation.

Think of a word that reflects the quality you wish to be filled with—relaxing, harmonizing, balancing, energizing, peace, patience, for example. See this particular quality as luminous energy which rises within you as you inhale, filling and flowing through you, completely permeating your mindbody. Allow this light-energy to dissolve all your negative states of mind, tension, or pain. Allow the natural vitality of life to awaken within you.

As you exhale, say to yourself "dissolving," "melting," "releasing," or "letting go." Feel the tensions, thoughts, cares, and painful states of mindbody flow out of you and melt away. Emphasize the long, slow exhalation, then allow the inhalation to come naturally, effortlessly.

Place your hands on your belly and quietly breathe in and out. Allow your belly to gently rise and fall as the breath flows through you.

After a few minutes, as the breath naturally fills your belly, allow it to rise up to the center of your chest and fill you as though a bubble of breath were filling you from within. Exhale through an imaginary hole in the center of your chest and allow your heart to open.

Breathing into your hands . . . bringing the air up to fill your heart . . . opening the heart . . . exhaling . . . opening and letting go.

THE SIMPLE NINE-PART BREATH

As a preliminary to meditation practice, some version or variation of the following concentration technique is recommended.

This involves alternating inhalations and exhalations through the left and right nostrils, as indicated below. You can close the opposite nostril with your thumb or index finger, or simply focus on one nostril at a time. Do not force or hold the breath, simply allow it to flow deeply, slowly, and at a natural rhythm.

1. Inhale right, exhale left (repeat three times each).
2. Inhale left, exhale right (repeat three times each).
3. Inhale both, exhale both (repeat three times each).

With each inhalation imagine drawing in pure, clear, vital energy in the form of light. Imagine it flowing through you, washing your senses and subtle bodies clean and clear. If you lose track of where you are in the sequence, return to the beginning and start again. Once you become familiar with this basic sequence, even visualizing this breath-flow pattern will be sufficient to bring about a sense of harmony and balance.

If you have difficulty breathing through your nose due to allergies or congestion, visualizing and imagining that your breath is moving through the nostrils in this way will often be an effective means of clearing your sinuses.

In addition to the image of inhaling pure white light or vital energy, the following visualization is also recommended to further balance and harmonize the mindbody:

1. As you exhale through the left nostril, imagine breathing out all your attachment and desire toward ideas, objects, perceptions, or states of mind. Visualize these as brownish red in color.

2. As you exhale through your right nostril, imagine breathing out all your anger, resentment, and frustration. Visualize these leaving your body in the form of inky dark smoke.

3. As you exhale through the both nostrils, imagine breathing out all your confusion, ignorance, pride, and any other mental states that obscure your perceptions and understanding of the true nature of

yourself and the world around you. Visualize these as clouds of darkness or fog.

Each time you inhale, breathe in light. As you exhale, imagine that all mental and emotional confusion, darkness and dullness of mind, dissolve completely into space, atomized and utterly gone. This is an excellent technique to apply frequently throughout the day, whenever you need to clear and focus your mind.

CONTEMPLATIVE PRACTICE

*Our discovery of God is in a way God's discovery of us.
We know Him in so far as we are known by Him, and
our contemplation of Him is a participation in God's contemplation of Himself. We become contemplative when
God discovers Himself in us. At that moment, the point of
our contact with God opens |up and we pass through the
center of our souls and enter eternity.*

—Thomas Merton

If you have a devotional orientation, the most effective object for your development of concentration might be a statue or image of a figure meaningful to you: Jesus, Mary, Buddha, a great saint, or a special teacher. Gazing at or visualizing one of these images or a sacred symbol, or reciting a prayer or mantra, can be very effective as a means for collecting your mind and bringing it to a calm state of concentration.

1. Select an object with special meaning.
2. Wholeheartedly devote your mind and body to this object for a chosen period of time.
3. Whenever your mind wanders, gently return it.

4. When you finish, relax, rejoice, and give thanks.

5. Carry over this calm and clarity into your next endeavor.

Allow yourself to go deeply into your contemplation. As you observe the object of concentration, let your mind settle upon it, relaxed yet alert. As you breathe in and out, feel a flow of energy and information between you and the essence of your object of contemplation. Let your mind move into it. Let its essential nature permeate you and reveal itself to you. Imagine, sense, or feel the essential truth of this image, mantra, sacred symbol, or prayer and let it resonate deep within you.

SPHERES OF MIND

Before me peaceful
Behind me peaceful
Under me peaceful
Over me peaceful
Around me peaceful
—Navajo blessing

Sit comfortably with your spine straight and your body relaxed. For a few minutes allow your attention to follow the breath or do the nine-part breath exercise (pages 67–69).

With your eyes closed or slightly open, reach out into the space in front of you and imagine that you are catching hold of a ball in the palm of your hand. Bring this imaginary ball closer to you and add a sense of vividness to its shape and size. Now imagine that instantaneously this transforms into a ball of brilliant white light, three-dimensional, transparent, luminous, lacking solidity. Imagine this ball of light radiating a sense of quiet calm and well-being. As you breathe, feel this ball of light come to rest at the center of your chest. Rest your attention here, effortlessly. Whenever it wanders, return to the inner visualization of a radiant sphere at the center of your chest.

If you feel a tightness in your chest when using this image, or your mind is too restless to focus, try the following variation:

Establish the image of a luminous sphere shining at the center of your chest. Now, regardless of what direction you are actually facing, mentally orient yourself as though you were facing east. Imagine that this sphere shoots straight out in front of you, beyond the eastern horizon to a place hundreds, thousands, even millions of miles away. Rest your mind on this sphere in the distant space. Experience the freedom of mind to reach out and extend itself farther and farther without limitation.

If your mind begins to lose interest or drift off into thoughts, once again establish the image of the radiant sphere at your chest. This time shift your attention to the western horizon behind you and vividly imagine sending the sphere out infinitely far in that direction. Rest your mind there. Again, when the mind wanders, reestablish the image at your heart.

With the next cycle, send the mind-sphere off to the southern direction to your right. Imagine the sphere hovering and radiating light thousands and millions of miles to your right. Allow the mind to rest there, undistracted and at ease. As before, when your attention wanders or fades, shift again, this time to focus on a sphere of light in space over the northern horizon to your left. With each phase of this practice, take as long over the visualization as feels comfortable.

Traditionally, you would continue with the horizon in front to the left and right, then behind you to your left and right, and even above and far below you. In any case, simply let the mind rest on this luminous sphere, this extension of your mind going out into the far distance. Spend as much time as you need to get a sense of the expansive, limitless nature of your mind.

Finally, expand your mind to encompass all the spheres you have sent out in all directions, along with the original one at your heart. Lucidly and effortlessly rest your mind in the experience of simultaneous expansion to all these directions.

Changing directions in this method introduces an element of novelty, freshness, and play. So wait until just before you have lost interest in the direction you are focusing on before changing to another. Remember that the purpose of this method is twofold: first, to stabilize, collect, and focus the mind upon what you are doing; and second, to introduce you to the open, luminous, unimpeded nature of your mind. If your mind were limited in its scope, how could it reach out to infinity in any direction you choose?

The expansive, luminous, knowing quality of your mind is not limited to the ordinary confines of your body and senses. It is unlimited, omnidirectional, able to reach out into any number of directions instantaneously. This method helps you to begin dispelling the misperception of your ordinary, limited sense-world. Try to practice frequently with these extraordinary mental muscles throughout the day.

CONCENTRATION WITH A NATURAL OBJECT

In a flash, the violent mind stood still.
Within, without are both transparent and clear.
After the great somersault,
the great void is broken through.
Oh, how freely come and go the myriad forms of things!
—Han Shan

Many of us have touched a state of deep concentration during times in nature. Watching the sunrise, sitting by a flowing stream, gazing upon a flower, a cloud, or raindrops on a still pool, our minds become clear, quiet, and deep. The chirp of crickets, the sound of breaking waves, or a babbling brook wash away our agitation and leave us calm and collected.

1. Select a natural object or process.
2. Attend to it wholeheartedly.
3. Open yourself to let it come in to you, and receive its light, sound, vibration, and life into yourself.
4. Open your heart and mind to embrace and be pervaded by it.
5. As you watch, listen, or feel this natural phenomenon, enter into a deep, quiet communion with it. Allow its essential nature and hidden qualities to reveal themselves intuitively.

CONCENTRATION WHILE WALKING

Much of our time in a day may be spent walking. This technique can help us to use walking as a means for developing concentration.

1. Count your first five steps.
2. With the next step, begin at one again and count up to six steps.
3. With the next step, begin at one again and count up to seven steps.
4. Continue counting in this way until you reach ten.
5. Now begin again, counting your steps from one to five.
6. Repeat the entire sequence up to ten steps as many times as you like.

If you lose track at any point (and you most likely will), begin again at the cycle of five steps. Note that if you begin on your right foot, the cycles ending in five and six steps will end on the right foot. Those ending at seven and eight will end on the left foot. And those ending at nine and ten will end on the right foot. This pattern will reverse with each full cycle. Remember the advice of a classic Zen poem that says, "When you walk, walk, and when you run, run. By all means don't wobble!"

> *There is a vitality, a life force, an energy, a quickening,*
> *that is translated through you into action, and because*
> *there is only one of you in all time, this expression is*
> *unique. And if you block it, it will never exist through*
> *any other medium and will be lost.*
>
> **—Martha Graham**

FOUR

MINDFULNESS MEDITATION:
THE CULTIVATION OF INSIGHT

MINDFULNESS IS THE PRACTICE OF making things real. It liberates us from memories of the past and fantasies of the future by bringing the reality of the present moment clearly into focus.

It is only in the present that we can come to clarity about what we are sensing, feeling, thinking, wanting, and willing to do. Elements of mindfulness meditation are found in all the world's great contemplative traditions. In the Buddhist tradition it is called "insight meditation" or *vipassana* (Sanskrit), which means "to see clearly."

As our mindfulness grows, we discover many exquisitely wonderful things about the world around us. Henry Miller once said, "The moment one gives close attention to anything, even a blade of grass, it becomes a mysterious, awesome, indescribably magnificent world in itself." With mindfulness we become more aware of life's everyday miracles and the awesome, subtle, intense, and exquisite, though transient, beauty of our world. As a result, our tender appreciation, gratitude, and compassion toward life and all living beings deepen.

Mindfulness also illuminates the discrepancies in our lives, so it takes courage to practice looking deeply into reality, to see ourselves and our world as they are. As we look deeply, moment to moment, we recognize what is not working and become more sensitive to the tension and suffering within ourselves, within others, and in our world. Mindfulness meditation opens our mind to more objectively behold the fleetingness of our joys and the immensities of the sorrows that come with life. It demagnetizes our fixations, our holding on to some experiences and pushing away others. As mindfulness grows we also begin to recognize more options, choices, resources, and opportunities in our lives. Synchronicities—meaningful coincidences—and insights become more a way of life.

Mindfulness gives rise to insights which ripen into wisdom, because the more deeply and clearly we are able to observe the reality of our mindbody and world, the more we will understand how and why things are as they are. As we come to a deeper understanding of ourselves, we come to a deeper understanding of our humanity. Our joys, sorrows, fears, or anger teach us about the joys, sorrows, fears, or anger of all beings. These insights ripen our empathy, patience, tolerance, and kindness—toward ourselves, and toward other living beings. Ane Pema Chödrön put it this way:

> Learning how to be kind to ourselves, learning how to respect ourselves, is important. The reason it's important is that, fundamentally, when we look into our own hearts and begin to discover what is confused and what is brilliant, what is bitter and what is sweet, it isn't just ourselves that we're discovering. We're discovering the universe.

While concentration meditation focuses our attention on a single, relatively stable object, mindfulness meditation assumes a more dynamic, inclusive field of observation. Traditionally, one first practices concentration meditation for some time to still and focus the wandering and undisciplined mind. Then this strong concentration is directed to look deeply into the nature of the mindbody process in order to awaken wisdom. Mindfulness meditation is then applied to investigate the nature of experience, and many profound insights arise that alter our deeply held, but unexamined, beliefs and realign our values with a way of life more in harmony with the deep nature of things.

THE BLESSING OF MINDFULNESS

With an eye made quiet by the power of
harmony and the deep power of joy
we see into the heart of things.

—William Wordsworth

The value of mindfulness is a universal theme found in all Eastern and Western wisdom traditions. In Western traditions, mindfulness is often associated with devotional practices in which we walk with God as our constant companion within us, or apprehend the presence of God. It has been described as looking at the world with the eyes of Christ's love, or as walking with Jesus by our side or within our deepest self at all times. In Jewish Kabbalah, the idea that creation is continually renewing itself moment to moment helps us bring a sense of wonder and awe into every moment, allowing each moment to be one of discovery and revelation. All these ideas can be practiced to raise our level of awareness and open our minds to behold our world as it really is.

THE BENEFITS OF MINDFULNESS

The rigor, objectivity, and insight gained through the practice of mindfulness have drawn thousands of scientists, psychologists, and researchers to this practice in recent decades; hundreds of studies have been launched to document the health and performance benefits of mindfulness meditation. Among the most well known of these is the Mindfulness Institute at the University of Massachusetts Medical Center, founded by Dr. Jon Kabat-Zinn.

When compared with the many problems caused by mindlessly living our lives, mindfulness helps us to:

- Improve focus, concentration, and precision.
- Enhance the quality of communications and relationships.
- Heighten the clarity of our thinking and intentions.
- Improve efficiency and safety.
- Deepen peace of mind and sense of flow.
- Master stress.
- Deepen insight and intuitive wisdom.
- Awaken more authenticity, heart, soul, and caring in our lives and work.
- Increase resilience to change.
- Strengthen faith and self-confidence.

THE WHEEL OF MINDFULNESS: THE WISDOM OF "WHOA!"

The "Wheel of Mindfulness" is a useful navigation tool to help you discover and describe to yourself what is true for you in each moment in each dimension of your being. Since the habit of mindlessness is stronger than the habit of mind-fulness, throughout the day you will often be totally lost in your thoughts. For this reason the quality of vigilance, discussed above in the section on concentration meditation, is a valuable ally in your practice of mindfulness meditation.

At times when your vigilance checks in only to find that mindlessness is afoot instead of mindful presence, say to yourself, "Whoa!" Let the "whoa" be sort of a fun "wake-up" call, inviting you to "come home to yourself." The "whoa!" helps you return to center and land squarely in the middle of the Wheel of Mindfulness. As you land in the center of the wheel, direct your attention to each of its spokes, asking yourself what is true for you in this moment: What am I noticing? What am I feeling? What are my thoughts? What do I need or want right now? What action is called for, or what am I willing to do?

The "whoa" gives you a simple mini-mindfulness practice that you can do throughout the day to come back to focus and center. For greater clarity in any situation, focus the beam of your mindfulness to check in with yourself—illuminating each of the following five domains:

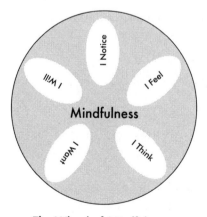

The Wheel of Mindfulness

I notice . . . Mindfulness of Perception and Action

In this moment of experience what do you notice going on? What is the raw sensory data available to you directly through the doorways of your sense perceptions—what do you see, hear, smell, touch, or taste that is happening in this situation? What you are looking to discover here is the kind of objective information that a video camera or tape recorder would pick up if they were recording this experience—with no overlay of judgment or interpretation.

I feel . . . Mindfulness of Emotional Feelings

How does this experience make you feel? Do you feel anxious or at ease, happy or sad, mad or glad, depressed or excited? What words best describe the emotional tone of your experience in this moment?

I think . . . Mindfulness of Thinking, Thoughts, and Imagination

What are your thoughts or "internal conversations" about your experience? Are you thinking creatively or are you merely replaying old thoughts?

What is the story you're telling yourself about a situation—your thoughts, fantasies, inferences, and assumptions? Recognizing old stories helps you to live more grounded in the reality of your present situation, and liberates you from mistaking your thoughts and assumptions for the reality that you are noticing!

I want . . . Mindfulness of Values, Motivations, Intentions, and Desires

What is your motivation or intention in this situation? What do you really want or need? Having clarity on your values, desires, intentions, and motivations is essential for effective communication and action.

I will . . . Moving Mindfulness into Action

What action are you willing to take in this situation?
What are you unwilling to do?
What are you willing to stop doing?

By knowing what you are perceiving, thinking, feeling, wanting, and intending in any given moment, you will be more
likely to recognize options, make wiser decisions, and to honestly and accurately communicate your experience to others.

Once you have reestablished mindfulness, then challenge yourself to carry that mindfulness back into action. If
you choose to make a phone call, mindfully enjoy the flow of
experience: your hand raising, moving, touching the phone,
lifting, dialing, deeply listening, speaking with mindfulness.
As you launch into action, be mindful of breathing, or walking, or thinking, or whatever action you have chosen.
Carrying mindfulness across the threshold of awareness into
the domain of action is key to transforming your life. When
you know what is true for yourself, you are better prepared
to communicate to others what you notice, feel, think, want,
and are willing to do. Rather than being a mindless slave
driven by unconscious habit, you will be more in control of
your life, more adaptable in the flow of change, and become
a conscious co-creator of your experience.

SELF-REMEMBERING

*If the heart wanders or is distracted, bring it back to the
point quite gently . . . and even if you did nothing during
the whole of your hour [of contemplation] but bring your
heart back, though it went away every time you brought
it back, your hour would be very well-employed.*

—Saint Francis de Sales

As you read these words, know that you are reading.

Developing our ability to be aware of what we are doing is called self-remembering. This practice enables us to fine-tune our perceptions and actions. It brings calm, clarity, and freedom to the mind, qualities that are necessary for recognizing the limiting patterns of habitual thought and actions, and for choosing more creative and effective options. With this awareness we can guide our lives toward attaining our goals.

> *As I breathe in, I know I am breathing in.*
> *Breathing out, I know I am breathing out.*
> *Listening, I know I am listening.*
> *Touching, I know I am touching.*
> *Lifting, I am aware of lifting.*
> *Sitting down, I am aware of sitting down.*
> *Thinking, I am aware of thinking.*
> *Experiencing fear, I am aware of feeling fear.*
> *Experiencing joy, I am aware of feeling joy.*
> *Intending, I am aware of intending.*
> *Beginning, I am aware of beginning.*
> *Reading, I am aware of reading.*
> *Finishing, I am aware of finishing.*

Suggestions:
   Mindfully go for a walk.
   Mindfully listen to music.
   Mindfully enjoy a meal.

Above all, keep your mind wholeheartedly on what you are doing. When it wanders—as it surely will—simply bring it back to what you are doing and, without self-criticism or lecturing yourself, return to your practice of self-remembering.

DOING WHAT YOU LOVE TO DO

*The first step in growth is to do what we
love to do and to become aware of doing it.*

—Sujata

What do you really enjoy doing? Have you ever considered that this could be an excellent meditation for you?

Doing what we love to do with mindful awareness can be a great place to begin the practice of meditation. The meditation is not the activity, but the quality of *attention* that we bring to the activity. Any activity of daily life can become a support for mindfulness meditation when it is undertaken with the intention of developing concentration, clarity, compassion, or insight.

1. Choose an activity you enjoy.

2. Determine to bring your full mindful attention to it.

3. Slowly, carefully, and mindfully begin. Stay relaxed and give your wholehearted attention to what you are doing.

4. Whenever your attention wanders or fades, gently return to being fully aware of what you are doing. If tension arises, relax and smile playfully to yourself.

5. When the activity or designated time period is over, pause for a few moments to reflect on the new richness you have discovered in this familiar activity.

In fact, everything that we do throughout the day, even the tasks that we do not like, can become a tool for developing our minds and deepening our concentration.

LISTENING

The more and more you listen, the more and more
you will hear. The more you hear, the
more and more deeply you will understand.

—Khyentse Rinpoche

For a simple and effective method to clear and focus your mind throughout the day, shift into a receptive listening mode. It is so quick and easy! "The mystery, the essence of all life is not separate from the silent openness of simple listening," says Zen teacher Toni Packer. Simply pause for a few minutes and be mindful of the sounds around you. Notice the phone ringing, horns honking, the sounds of voices, the roar of traffic, the chirping of birds. Let your mind be like a sensitive antenna—a listening, receptive space of awareness in which sounds come and go, rising and falling into silence. Let your listening awareness effortlessly receive sound like an ocean receives rain or earth receives water. Without needing to think about them, just let the sounds come and flow. The moment you notice that you've spun off into thinking, smile to yourself and mentally say: "Listen. . . ." Notice how all sounds come out of silence . . . and dissolve back into silence. Notice how your listening mind is like the deep, clear sky which can contain limitless different sounds without any of them getting in the way. Just breathe, listen, and smile for a few deep, refreshing moments.

LISTEN . . .
We are continually hearing information
   from the world around and within us.
     Minimize distortion by turning down the
      volume of your internal dialogue.

Imagine that the universe is about
to whisper the answer to your deepest
questions . . . and you don't want to miss it!

LISTEN . . .
Simply, and without analysis or commentary to
whatever sounds enter the sphere of your
awareness. Don't label the sounds. If you
start thinking, remind yourself to just . . .

LISTEN . . .
Effortlessly to sounds.
Let them come to you.
No need to tense or strain.
Trust. Let go of control. Be at ease.
Still . . . quiet . . . receptive . . . and alert.

LISTEN . . .
Notice how sounds arise . . . and fade away . . .
Melting into silence or into other sounds.
Don't try to hold them, allow them to flow . . .

LISTEN . . .
Where do the sounds go?

LISTEN . . .
Where do the sounds come from?

LISTEN . . .
Experience how the space of your awareness
effortlessly accommodates an interpenetrating
symphony of sounds, thoughts, sensations, feelings,
and visions simultaneously. Allow your
mindbody to relax into unencumbered clarity . . .

LISTEN . . .
Allow the answers to these questions to
come as understanding, not as thoughts.

LISTEN . . .
And reflect . . .
   Who is listening? . . .

If you pause for a few minutes of mindful listening like this throughout the day, you'll be amazed at how clear and calm your mind becomes. And like many of the other methods in this book, you can practice listening anytime and in any place. For example, you might be sitting in your office or waiting for a bus. While there may be a fair amount of activity and chaos around you, you can still find your quiet center even in the midst of all this activity. As you practice these methods in simple, quiet times, it will be easier to access them when things are more chaotic.

MINDFULNESS OF BREATHING

Breathing in I calm my body and mind,
Breathing out I smile.
Breathing . . . smiling. . . .

—Thich Nhat Hanh

The technique of mindful breathing is very simple: As you inhale, know that you're breathing in. . . . As you exhale, know that you're breathing out. . . . As you rest in the awareness of your breathing, mindfully experience the moment-to-moment flow of sensations as the breath flows in and out of your nostrils, or as your abdomen naturally rises and falls.

The more effortlessly and naturally you ride the waves of your breath, the more effective this technique will be. This exercise is not intended to control or change your breath in any way. It isn't about breathing deeper or slower or trying to manipulate the breath at all, as in some yoga or deep breathing exercises. In fact, strictly speaking, it isn't even an "exercise" but a simple focusing of awareness into what is already going on naturally by itself. In essence, we let go of trying to control and allow the power of awareness to do the balancing work by itself. Simply relax into your breath, feeling it just as it is. About 21,600 times a day, you have the opportunity to catch the wave of your breath: mindfully inhaling . . . mindfully exhaling . . . with a gentle smile and full awareness.

Mindful breathing accomplishes one of the greatest |miracles of life—it brings your mind and body into synch with each other and into clear focus so that your body-mind-spirit can work together with balanced presence. Since mental functioning and quality of consciousness are so closely related to the way you're breathing, practicing mindful breathing can have a focusing, calming, and vitalizing effect for your whole mind and body.

As a technique for balancing energy, focusing on the rising and falling movement of your abdomen is especially effective. Follow your breath and simply notice the natural rising and falling sensations of the movement itself. In this way, mindful breathing can become a centering pulse of focusing and flowing attention, creating a wave of awareness that you can ride to help steady yourself through every activity of your life. With mindfulness of breathing as your home base, you can focus your attention and direct it to observe anything or to perform any action with greater presence and equipoise. Each breath focusing . . . and flowing. Focusing . . . and flowing. . . .

STILL-POINTS

As you mindfully observe the flow of your breathing, you will discover that in the midst of the flow of change there are still-points. These are revealed at the very climax of the inhalation, before the exhalation begins, and again at the bottom of the exhalation before the next inhalation begins. Taking this observation to heart, you may discover the wisdom of pausing to collect yourself, fully focus your attention, or get clear on your intention after you finish something before starting the next thing. With practice, you can learn to be more fully present with change by building frequent pauses into your busy day. These needn't be long in duration, but the more frequently we stop, scan, and tune ourselves toward a more balanced state, the more we will be able to bring greater flow, sensitivity, wisdom, and care into the moments that follow.

Building more still-points into your life provides a welcome opportunity to harvest insights and apply them. This is like pausing to push the "clear" button on your calculator after numerous computations have started to get confusing. A blank slate allows you to begin again, fresh and clear.

MINDFULNESS OF YOUR BODY: MENTAL MASSAGE

The second base of mindfulness is to be mindful of your body. Right now as you sit here, become aware of your posture. Notice the sensations of your hands touching, holding the book, or resting in your lap. Notice the sensations of your bottom on the seat. Smile to yourself as you come out of the clouds of your thoughts and land with full awareness in your body.

Throughout the day, one of the simplest ways of getting focused and mastering stress is to become mindful of the position of your body. If you're mindful of your body frequently throughout the day, you'll begin to recognize the accumulation of tension sooner and be better able to let it go more easily and swiftly. As a result, you'll be less likely to build up a lot of tension and, therefore, less likely to develop stress-related illnesses. In this way, mindfulness is the basic foundation of preventive medicine.

There's a very simple, powerful method for weaving body awareness into your daily life. As you breathe, feel the rising and falling of your chest or abdomen. Feel the stream of sensations as the breath flows into and out of your nostrils. At the top of the inhalation, in the pause, tune in to a "touch point"—notice your bottom touching the chair, or the sensations of your hands or your lips touching. Then ride the wave of sensations of the outflowing breath, and at the bottom of the exhalation, again tune in to a touch point, a moment of mindfulness of your body.

Another way to strengthen body mindfulness is by sweeping your awareness through your body. One way to do this is to begin at the top of your head and as you breathe, allow your inhalations to focus your attention in this region. Simply be aware of any sensations or vibrations that you experience here. Then allow your mindful attention to travel slowly down through your body, breath by breath, and part by part. When your awareness reaches your toes, then gently return your attention to the top of your head and once again let your awareness sweep down through your body, lighting each part up with awareness.

Welcome whatever comes to your attention. If what you encounter is pleasurable or painful, let those feelings flow into and through your awareness of the present, ever-changing moment. Let your mindfulness flow through your body like a warm wave or gentle breeze passing through an icefield, or like a pure light shining through a dark crystal. As the warm light of your awareness sweeps through your body, allow the blocks of tension to melt, soften, and release. Like a magnet passing over a pile of jumbled iron filings, with each pass through your body, feel subtler dimensions of your body beginning to align and flow more smoothly and harmoniously. Pay particular attention to how these subtle sensations change, how everything inside you is moving, vibrating, changing moment to moment.

With practice you will refine your sensitivity to be able to sense, feel, and actually alter the patterns of subtle sensation and energy through the power of your awareness. As you sweep your tender awareness through your body, allow it to flow particularly through regions of discomfort or disease. Gently direct the mind to sweep back and forth, up and down, moving like a laser beam or a floodlight, sweeping from different directions, front to back, top to bottom, diagonally or in spirals. Intuitively feel how you can best move your attention into a region of internal space and try different approaches until no obstruction or resistance remains. Though at first the body may seem riddled with discomfort or some regions may be impossible to sense or feel at all, gradually these parts of yourself will come alive with sensations and feelings of a more harmonious resonance. As your mindfulness of your body deepens, it will reveal a treasury of profound insights to you.

INVESTIGATING THE MIND

One should realize that one does not meditate in order to
go deeply into oneself and withdraw from the world. . . .
There should be no feeling of striving to reach some exalted
or higher state, since this simply produces something con-
ditioned and artificial that will act as an obstruction to
the free flow of the mind. . . . When performing the medi-
tation practice, one should develop the feeling of opening
oneself out completely to the whole universe with absolute
simplicity and nakedness of mind. . . . Meditation is not to
develop trance-like states; rather it is to sharpen percep-

tions, to see things as they are. Meditation at this level is
relating with the conflicts of our life situations, like using
a stone to sharpen a knife, the situation being the stone.

—*Trungpa Rinpoche*

There are many objects of meditation. While some traditions may emphasize a physiological process such as breath or posture, others focus attention on the changing nature of thoughts, feelings, sensations, emotions, and states of consciousness.

Within the mind we experience a ceaseless flow of mental, emotional, and sensory experiences. Ordinarily our attention wanders a lot, we are lost in our thoughts and only superficially aware of what is taking place within or around us. With mindful observation of our experience, we grow more sensitive to what we are perceiving, feeling, thinking, and doing. More in touch with ourselves, we are more in touch with the world. Old reactive patterns fall away, revealing the natural power, wisdom, and love that is the mind's true nature.

The following sequence of exercises is excellent for developing insight into how your mind works. For best results, practice the first exercise for a few days or weeks until you have gained some insight, then move on to the next, until eventually you have completed the sequence.

1. Noting Sensory Experiences

   Begin as in the previous exercises, using the breath to help stabilize and focus your mind. Now, expand your ability to notice your mental process by including sensory experiences. Whenever you become aware of physical sensation, either make the mental note "feeling" or, if you want to be more specific, "pleasure," "pain," "tingling," "itching," etc. Do not engage in internal dialogue, but simply and crisply note what you are experiencing and bring your awareness back to your breath. Likewise, when you become aware of other sensory experiences, note "hearing," "tasting," "smelling," "touching."

2. Noting Emotional Feelings
Begin by relaxing your body and focusing your mind with a few moments of watching the breath flow. Then, in addition to noting sensory experiences, also note your emotional experiences. Whenever a particular feeling predominates, note its nature, such as "anger," "sadness," "fear," "resentment," "guilt," "anxiety," or whatever brief mental label fits. Pay particular attention to experiences of "liking" and "disliking." Once again, do not become involved with the content of the emotions, simply note them and return to awareness of the breath.

3. Mindfulness of Thoughts
Jack Kornfield states, "In the development of wisdom, one quality of mind above all others is the key to practice. This quality is mindfulness, attention, or self-recollection. The most direct way to understand our life situation, who we are and how our mind and body operate, is to observe with a mind that simply notices all events equally. This attitude of non-judgmental, direct observation allows all events to occur in a natural way. By keeping the attention in the present moment, we can see more and more clearly the true characteristics of our mind and body process."

This is a meditation using thoughts. Though many people experience thoughts as a distraction to meditation practice, thoughts can make an interesting and effective object of meditation in themselves. By making thoughts the object of our attention we come to the profound understanding that we are not our thoughts. We realize that thoughts are merely bubbles floating in the vast ocean of the mind, or clouds that arise, change, and pass in the sky of mind. By learning to consciously disidentify from the contents of our thoughts, we learn to view thinking as a process that will arise and unfold without the need of a "thinker." Looking deeply into our thoughts of who we are, we find we are far more and greater than all the voices and ideas that arise and pass in the mind's open, clear space.

Begin by sitting quietly and attending to the natural inflow and outflow of the breath. As thoughts arise, make a mental note: "thinking . . . thinking." Once recognized, many "trains of thought" will be derailed and the mind will once again become quiet. Practice noticing the thoughts quickly, before they have swept you off into association and elaboration. As the thoughts subside, simply return to attending to the flow of breath.

Having built a foundation of mindfulness with your breath and body, the next base of mindfulness to develop is mindfulness of thinking. According to some researchers, as many as 90% of the thoughts we think are "reruns" of thoughts we've already thought before!

You can learn to simply and heartfully watch the changing images and listen to the endless flow of inner voices without needing to get involved in them. However, this is not as easy as it sounds. If you're like most people, you've spent your whole life identifying with these voices, and struggling with them without really considering that these thoughts are only thoughts, and really have little power over you unless you give it to them. Your real source of balance lies in remembering that you are more than the chatter you hear in your head. You are also the presence of mind that knows these thoughts, and the space of awareness in which all these many thoughts coalesce and dissolve. When we hold our thoughts lightly, like wispy cloud formations dancing in the deep, clear sky of mind, we are able to see through them to the creative intelligence that underlies and sustains them.

With mindfulness and a compassionate, patient smile, you can choose which thoughts or voices to follow and which to merely let pass by. This smile will protect you from taking any of these voices too seriously, trying too hard, or being too judgmental, as you learn to sit quietly by the stream of your mind. Here are a series of exercises to increase your mindfulness of thoughts:

a. Labeling Thoughts

For some people, labeling the different kinds of thought processes is helpful. When memories arise in the mind, note "remembering." When fantasies of the future arise, note "imagining" or "planning." Such labeling can help to strengthen the focus and clarity of the mind and help you to identify and dissect the predominant patterns of thought you have compulsively identified with and been impelled by throughout your life. In learning to simply recognize thinking as thinking, planning as planning, blaming as blaming, remembering as remembering, we begin to find our power in the present moment and free ourselves from the prison of misidentifying with the limiting patterns of our thoughts. In this way, the power of our minds can be understood and properly directed toward energizing the development of the deeper qualities of human beingness.

As you practice this meditation, guard against identifying with the content of your thoughts. Simply pay close attention to the *process* of thinking. Pay particular attention to the compulsive and reflexive tendency to generate thoughts about your thoughts and engage in inner commentary about them. Don't regard thoughts as either good or bad, right or wrong, or as hindrances to your meditation practice. As the great contemporary Zen master Shunryu Suzuki Roshi wrote in his now classic book, Zen Mind, Beginners Mind:

When you are practicing zazen meditation, do not try to stop your thinking. Let it stop by itself. If something comes into your mind, let it come in and let it go out. It will not stay long. When you try to stop your thinking, it means you are bothered by it. Do not be bothered by anything. It appears that the something comes from outside your mind, but actually it is only the waves of your mind and if you are not bothered by the waves, gradually they will become calmer and calmer. . . . Many sensations come, many thoughts and images arise but they are just waves from your own mind. Nothing comes from outside your mind. . . . If you leave your mind as it is, it will become calm. This mind is called Big Mind.

b. Memories and Fantasies

Begin by sitting quietly and focusing your attention with a few moments of mindful breathing. Build the strength and continuity of your attention by breathing your mindful awareness into this moment, and letting it continue as an unbroken stream of awareness into this next moment. Each moment and each breath, stay fully focused and mindfully present.

Now, rest your hands on your knees: right hand on your right knee, left hand on your left knee. As you breathe, draw your attention to mindfully focus on the stream of your thoughts. Staying mindful of each moment, whenever you notice a thought that's a memory of the past, tap gently with your left hand, indicating to yourself that you're aware of a special kind of thought called a memory. If you like, you can anchor it by saying mentally to yourself, "memory." Whenever you notice you're having a thought that's a fantasy of the future, tap your right knee and if you like, mentally note, "fantasy." With the mind calm yet alert, watch the breath flow, simply noting the excursions of your mind into past memories and future fantasies. As thoughts arise, mentally note "memory" or "fantasy," then return your attention to the flow of the breath.

As thoughts arise, view them simply as clouds floating through the sky of your mind, or as different taxicabs racing here and there in the mind. Remember not to hitch a ride on any of them! Avoid the tendency to mindlessly climb aboard and get lost in the thoughts. Simply let them come and go. Stay mindfully focused, and keep tapping your left knee for thoughts of the past and your right knee for thoughts of the future.

After a few minutes, reflect to yourself, "Has my attention been drawn more to memories of the past, to fantasies or plans for the future, or balanced more in the present?" Objectively, with the desire to learn and without criticism, simply notice which ways your attention is most drawn.

As your powers of mindfulness grow, you'll gain more insight into how your mind works. Understanding more about your patterns of attention, you'll come to a clearer recognition of the patterns of mind that you'd like to strengthen as well as the patterns of mind you'd like to reduce.

c. Pleasant, Unpleasant, and Neutral Experiences

Now, as you watch the flow of experience passing through your mind, be mindful of three kinds of experiences. When these are feelings, you can label them "pleasant," "unpleasant," or "neutral." When these experiences are thoughts, you might note, "liking or enjoying," "disliking," or "neutral." When you notice judging thoughts that are associated with "unpleasant feelings," mark them by tapping your left knee. When you notice experiences that trigger "pleasant" feelings, tap your right knee. When you're in a neutral, aware quality of experience, just sit quietly and mindfully enjoy the experience of your breathing and the flow of neutral thoughts and feelings.

Once again, avoid the tendency to dive in and get carried away or caught up with the content of your thoughts. Simply notice and be mindful of the tendencies activated in your thinking process. Ultimately, you'll learn to be mindful of whatever you're thinking, and by being more mindful of what you're thinking, you'll be able to direct your thinking as you wish.

5. Noting and Noticing the Changing State of the Mind

As the mind becomes more stable and balanced, the practice of labeling or noting thoughts, emotions, or phases of the breath may begin to feel cumbersome. Once you have reached this level of mental subtlety, begin to simply notice the inhalation or exhalation, or the type of thought or emotional state, without generating a mental label. The practice of mindfully noticing myriad arising and passing thoughts, physical sensations, emotional feelings, and states of consciousness allows the mind to penetrate more deeply into the essential nature of these experiences.

If you find that the clarity or precision of your attention begins to fade, simply return to breath awareness or mental noting techniques in order to sharpen the focus of your attention. Once mental clarity and lucidity have been reestablished, let go of noting and return to simply *noticing* the ever-changing flow of states of mind and body which are woven into the fabric of your experience.

6. Intention

Once you have become familiar with recognizing your thoughts and feelings as they arise, you will be able to see that prior to every voluntary action there is a mental intention. Becoming more mindful of your intentions will strengthen your mindfulness in action. This is a very powerful way to learn more about how your mind works. For example, when you're driving, be watchful for how your intention to change lanes, turn left or right, or slow down or speed up precedes your actual actions.

Begin now to notice this intending phase of your experience. Mentally note the intention to stand up before getting off a chair; the intention to reach out before you open a door. Note the intention to move, to stop, to speak, to turn, to speed up or slow down, to be harsh, or to be kind.

When you're sitting somewhere, the idea may come to your mind to go get something that's in another room. When this happens, instead of instantly jumping up on "automatic pilot," immediately recognize the thoughts and the images as they arise in your mind and sense the impulse to get up and go get the object. Feel this intention to act—to stand and walk into the next room—moving in your body. Then, if you so choose, in a relaxed and fully present way mindfully stand up and walk into the other room, pick up the object, and return. Throughout this entire sequence of inner and outer movement, remain balanced in mindfulness and let the continuity of your attention be unbroken.

By developing mindfulness of intention, we can develop greater power for creative choice, for seeing a whole new range of options that we hadn't seen before and that are available to us in spite of the habitual and highly conditioned mode most of us live in. As you develop insight into the often unconscious and habitual impulses that direct your behavior, you will discover even greater freedom and power to choose both what you do and how you do it. The old Zen poem speaks to this clarity and power of intentionality in action:

> When you walk, walk!
> When you run, run!
> By all means, don't wobble!

In the fast pace of daily life, inevitably you will get caught up and carried along by habitual and conditioned thoughts and emotional feelings, and lose your focus of attention and the ability to consciously choose what to do or say. When you become aware of this, mentally stop, smile to yourself, perhaps even chide yourself playfully—and then breathe and allow your thoughts and feelings to move and flow and your sense of strength, calmness, and clarity to grow.

7. Mindfulness of the Stories We Tell Ourselves
The major cause of stress for most people arises from self-generated anxiety and worries. Since the body responds equally to mental images as to sensory ones, learning to monitor and sort through our thoughts can be a major step toward inner peace.

Here's a mindfulness of thought technique that comes from a tribe in Africa. From an early age, children in this tribe are trained to be mindful of their thinking. If a person becomes aware of a foreboding thought like, "Oh no, what if there is a lion hiding behind that tree waiting to eat me?" they learn first to recognize and then release the thought by acknowledging to themselves, "This is a story that doesn't need to happen!"

We use this technique often. For example, one of us may be chopping veggies with a sharp knife and the thought pops up, "I'd better be careful or I'll cut myself," or, in a rush driving on the freeway, an image of getting pulled over by the Highway Patrol flashes into our mind. The key is to first notice the thought and then, if it is harmful or unproductive, to say to yourself, "This is a story that doesn't need to happen." This technique is not about getting rid of negative thoughts or about the power of positive thinking. If a stress-inducing "doom and gloom" kind of thought comes to mind, acknowledge it, don't try to get rid of it, hold on to it, or even analyze it. Simply honor it and let it go.

This dynamic meditation on the flow of thoughts is also useful in recognizing that some of those stories that pop into our minds are ones we'd *like* to see happen. In response to a desirable mental scenario, such as, "Maybe there is a watering hole over there," or "I hope the baby I am carrying will be healthy and grow to be a leader," the members of this tribe would say to themselves, "And this is a healing story!" In your life you might bless or energize such thoughts as "I know I'll do a great job on that presentation," "This meal is going to be delicious," or "This lump is probably benign" by thinking or saying, "Yes, and this is a healing story."

In our work with leaders and teams, we often teach this technique as a way of strengthening mind-fulness of our unconscious, and often self-sabotaging, inner dialogue. Many people have found it very simple and useful. Recognizing your flow of thoughts will help you smile to yourself and get play-fully creative. For example, if you notice thoughts like, "I'll never get this done," "I'll mess this up," "They'll think I'm incompetent," or "My presentation will be a bomb," it may be helpful to smile to yourself and say, "This is a story that doesn't need to happen." And if you notice thoughts like, "My client will love this design," or "People are really going to love this idea!" anchor them by affirming, "And this is a healing story!"

KITCHEN YOGI MEDITATION

The technique that follows was inspired by the insight that all daily life activities can be transformed into meditations, even the most mundane and ordinary ones, such as washing and chopping vegetables. The key to this transformation lies in the art of paying close attention to whatever is happening in the present moment. It is not the activity that determines the quality of mental aliveness, but rather the energy of mindfulness we bring to it. We spend much of our lives doing routine and mechanical chores. Experiment with these guidelines to see how you can transform whatever you are doing into an experience of wakefulness.

- Begin by grounding yourself. Feel the contact between the soles of your two feet and the floor. Note the feeling of your feet touching the ground and sense how the floor beneath you connects you to the earth.
- With your knees slightly bent, feel your legs growing down into the earth, your hips, thighs, and legs growing down into the earth.
- Move your awareness next into your navel at the center of your body.
- Now allow the upper part of your body to open and become alive. As you exhale allow your shoulders

to drop. With each exhalation, let your eyes soften and your jaw be loose and soft.

- With each exhalation come back to your body. Sense your body posture.
- Be receptive. Allow the visual sensation of the vegetable to come to you as you chop with the knife.
- There is nothing to do but feel the sensation of the knife in your hand. Feel its hardness. Become aware of the sensation of contact, the touch of your hand on the knife. Are you squeezing more than you need to as you chop? Soften your grip.
- Allow the feeling of the vegetable you are holding to come to you. Note the quality of the sensation.
- Feet touching the floor.
- Knees slightly bent.
- Moving from the center.
- Be aware of the breath.
- Eyes soft.
- Open and receptive.
- Stay in touch with the flow of sensations.
- Attend to every moment as if it were your first . . . or last.
- Alert . . . relaxed and precise.
- Mindfully moving from moment to moment.

MINDFUL EATING

Every activity of your life provides an opportunity to strengthen the power of your mindfulness. Since eating is something that you do a number of times each day, mindful eating can give you another tool to polish your awareness and invite more moments of mindful presence into your daily life.

Practicing mindfulness of eating can be very revealing. There are many processes going on in the mind and body while we eat. As we bring our attention to the sequence of these processes, deep self-understanding can arise. For example, the first step in eating is seeing the food. Begin by simply smiling to yourself, and become aware of "seeing." Let that steaming bowl of soup or juicy sandwich become "real" to you. Feel your hunger and notice also the smell of the food you're about to eat.

The next step is intending to reach for it. Become aware of this. The intention drives the body into action to reach for the food. When you're ready, mindfully reach out and make contact with the food. Again, become aware of the process of "reaching or moving." When your hand or fork touches the food, there is the sensation of touching. Be aware of this experience of touching. Feel the sensations as you touch the apple or sandwich. Next, raise your arm, lifting the food into your mouth. Be mindful of the experience of lifting it to your mouth and of your mouth opening. As you put the food into your mouth, be mindful of the touch of the food on your tongue and the burst of taste lighting up your mouth.

Carefully notice each phase of the process. As the food comes toward your mouth, notice opening the mouth, putting the food in, lowering the arm, feeling the texture of the food in the mouth, chewing and tasting. Mindfully chew your food and feel the blending of textures and tastes dancing around your mouth. Be particularly mindful of the experience of tasting. Notice how, as you chew, the taste disappears. Then, when you're ready, be mindful of swallowing. If you have time, pause for a mindful breath or two before going on to the next mouthful. Notice the sensations of hunger as well as any feelings of compulsiveness that might drive you to shovel in another mouthful even before you've finished the first one. Take control of these raging forces that often unconsciously control your life. Watch how desire for more arises, leading to the intention to reach for another bite. Then again be mindful of seeing, smelling, intending, reaching, touching, lifting, opening, tasting, chewing, swallowing, and enjoying.

Experience how one phase seems to mechanically lead to the next as though there is really no one eating, only a sequence of related events unfolding: intention, movement, touch sensations, tastes, etc. Mindful eating can reveal how what we are is just a sequence of happenings, a process and flow of life-energy. It can also mirror to us many of our compulsive attitudes toward consuming the universe or receiving nourishment through all of our senses. As we learn to step back and notice the process as well as the content of our activities, we can begin to recognize and transform many old, limiting patterns and choose new and more creative options for how to live our lives.

You may be surprised by how much you can learn about yourself by eating a meal mindfully now and then. Since hunger is controlled by the hypothalamus, the small master organ in the core brain or limbic system, the same part of your brain that regulates stress response, emotions, and sexuality, practicing mindful eating may also provide you with some very interesting insights into other areas of your life as well.

Keeping in mind that we nourish—and undernourish—ourselves in many ways, you may find that being mindful of eating may offer you valuable understanding into how you assimilate many other kinds of information in your life. For example, how fully present are you to receive and taste the sweetness of things that you've "cooked up" and put a lot of energy into creating? Are the choices that you're making really nourishing you? How well are you chewing and assimilating the information you put on your plate in other arenas of your life? Are you suffering from information indigestion? The same discomfort that leads you to reach for another bite of food while your mouth is still full may offer insights into patterns that prevent you from fully savoring or understanding complex relationships in your job or your family.

Becoming more mindful in your life will reveal patterns that promote self-development, and other patterns that are self-sabotaging. As you cultivate mindfulness, remember to keep a tender smile with you. This smile is a reminder of your objectivity, your own tenderness, mercy, and compassion. This is also the smile of your courage and inner strength that is willing to look deeply enough at your life to recognize what's really there.

MINDFUL WALKING

Every path, every street in the world
is your walking meditation path.

—Thich Nhat Hanh

Walking meditation provides a welcome method for bringing the meditative mind into action. Though at first it may be easier for you to become mindful of your breathing, thinking, and surroundings when there isn't a lot going on around you, you'll find that the real power of mindfulness is to be found in taking mindfulness into action.

One of the simplest ways to do this is to practice walking mindfully. Mindful walking is an important method of focusing your attention while you're moving. In our work with the U.S. Army Green Berets we used to call this "power-walking" because mind and body, energy and intention, are all focused together. To get a feeling for this, begin by just walking very slowly and mindfully. Once you get a feeling for it you can practice mindful walking at any pace in any place.

Mindfulness reveals that just as sound begins and ends in silence, movement begins and ends in stillness. So to begin, first feel yourself standing still. Focus your mindful attention with the breath and smile knowingly to yourself. Then, when you're ready to walk, notice how you shift your balance and weight to one foot, and then feel the other foot lifting . . . and feel the foot moving, touching the ground . . . then feel your weight and balance shift again.

You can see that each step has four phases: shifting . . . lifting . . . moving . . . placing. Being very present, very mindful, you walk and know each step of your walking. At first you may find it helpful to make a mental note for each part of the step, thinking or saying softly to yourself, "lifting . . ." "moving . . ." "placing . . ." "shifting. . . ." Once your mind quiets down and gets more focused, you can let go of noting the movements and simply notice them.

When you practice mindful walking, the goal is not to get somewhere or to accomplish something. The goal is to simply, fully arrive in each moment, with each step. Your measure of success is in how fully present you are with what you're doing. If you understand this, you can practice mindful walking in your own living room. Slowly, with full awareness, walk across the room, turn around with full awareness and walk back across the room. Rather than pacing back and forth, you're actually bringing your mind and body into focus, which means that whatever you turn your attention to next, you'll be able to be more fully present and think with greater clarity and power.

Once you have a feeling for mindful walking, you can practice everywhere you go and at any pace. When walking briskly, you might notice, "step . . . step . . . step . . . ." or "left . . . right . . . left . . . right." Or even "arriving . . . home . . ." or "here . . . and now . . . ." Be mindful of your whole body as you walk and remember to smile, relax, and let the breath flow naturally. See if you can bring a quality of tenderness to your steps, as if you're planting a flower that will spring up and bloom wherever you place your feet, or as if each footstep brings a blessing to the earth. When distractions arise, smile to yourself, acknowledge them without getting involved, and continue your mindful walking.

Mindful walking is an excellent method of meditation, especially at times when the mind is agitated and it is difficult to sit quietly. Start off slowly. Begin by noticing the sequence of movements as you walk: standing, lifting, moving, placing one foot, shifting your weight. Then lift, move, place, and shift your weight to the other foot. Move no faster than you are able to with complete awareness. This is not a moving meditation so much as an exercise in developing continuity of mindful awareness. At times, experiment with walking more swiftly, simply noting each time a foot touches the ground. Be loose and natural. Experience the flow of movement, moment to moment, with awareness.

Remember, the goal is not to get somewhere. Each moment you are fully present in the flow of movement, you have arrived at your destination.

SITTING IN THE FIRE:
BEARING WITNESS TO SUFFERING
WITH COMPASSIONATE AWARENESS

*There's an interesting transition that occurs
naturally and spontaneously. We begin to find that,
to the degree that there is bravery in ouselves—the will-
ingness to look, to point directly at our own hearts—
and to the degree that there is kindness toward
ourselves, there is confidence that we can actually
forget ourselves and open to the world.*

—Ane Pema Chödrön

The heart of mindfulness is compassionate awareness able to hold and bear any experience without turning away, and without compulsively trying to change the experience. Developing our capacity to "sit in the fire" with our own suffering is very powerful. Thich Nhat Hanh reminds us that we need to remember to "smile to our sorrow and to our pain because we are more than our sorrow or pain." Finding the courage to "sit in the fire" also builds our confidence and compassion and strengthens us to be more wholeheartedly present with others we care for when they are suffering.

First, center and balance yourself by mindfully resting in the flow of your breathing. Inhaling, gently smile to yourself and know that you are breathing in.

Exhaling, gently smile to yourself and know that you are breathing out.

Inhaling ... exhaling ... mindfully with full awareness of the sensations of the breath flow.

After a few moments of centering yourself with mindful breathing, turn your mindfulness to deeply experience whatever discomfort may be present for you.

Allow the steadiness of your mindful breathing to help you to draw your awareness into the experience, and then carefully observe in minute detail the nature of the sensations, emotional feelings, thoughts, and perceptions that you find here.

Then make a mental note of whatever you are experiencing: "itching ... itching ..." "burning ... burning ..." restlessness ... restlessness ... " "worry ... worry ..." "anger ... anger ..." "fear ... fear ..." or whatever best describes your experience in the moment. Allow the breath and the gentle smile to steady your awareness as you go.

Gradually allow your mindfulness to investigate how this experience is changing and modulating in nature and intensity moment to moment. Notice how this experience that you label with a certain concept is actually a constellation of ephemeral, constantly changing phenomena.

Notice the flow and patterns of sensations in your body that are associated with a physical pain, emotional upset, or state of mind. With an inquiring mind notice: Are the sensations pulsing, throbbing, tingling, intense, subtle, painful, pleasurable, steady?

In a similar way, focus your mindfulness to investigate the changing nature of emotional feelings: What physical sensations are linked to this emotional experience? Is this emotional state constant, changing, intense, subtle? What thoughts or inner conversations are associated with these emotional feelings and physical sensations? Looking, listening, and feeling deeply into the moment, discover what is really taking place without imposing extra overlay or interpretation upon it. Allow your mindfulness to give rise to insight into the nature of suffering, its causes and conditions, its changing nature, its gifts and challenges, and allow a greater wisdom and compassion to grow through the power of your presence.

MINDFUL DIALOGUE:
THE PRACTICE OF DEEP LISTENING
AND MINDFUL SPEECH

We spend much of our time talking with people, so deep listening and mindful speaking is a perfect meditation practice for us to learn and practice in daily life. So much joy and suffering come through how we communicate, so learning to bring greater awareness and sensitivity to talking with others is a very important skill. The spirit of this meditation is found in the following series of gestures:

First, reach out with both hands and imagine that this indicates that all of your attention is focused outwardly and that you are not in touch with yourself.

Second, bring both hands to your heart in a gesture that indicates that you are really in touch with yourself, but have little or no attention going to others or to the world around you.

Next, leave one hand at your heart as an affirmation of deep awareness and connectedness with yourself—you know what is true for you and what you are perceiving, feeling, thinking, wanting, and willing to do. With your other hand reach out and imagine that this hand indicates your attention to and engagement with others and the world around you.

The key now is to hold this last gesture inwardly as you engage in dialogue with someone. This gesture of mindfulness allows you to be in touch and deeply listening both to yourself and to whomever you are talking with. As the conversation continues, maintain your mindfulness of what is taking place inside you—what you are feeling, and thinking, and wanting, etc.—while being completely present and attentive to you partner.

This meditation can be done with people who haven't a clue that they are actually the focus of your mindfulness meditation, and they will likely be grateful for the experience. This can also be shared in an intentional way with a partner who is also cultivating deep listening and mindful speaking. In this case, add to these guidelines an invitation for either of you at any time to simply call "whoa," at which time you both pause, stop speaking, and, in a sense, bring your hands back to your hearts and check in with how this experience is impacting you. After a few quiet moments, reengage and continue your conversation, speaking, if you like, to the insights you may have just come to when checking in with yourself.

PEBBLE MEDITATION

This is a wonderful meditation practice for children we learned from Thich Nhat Hanh. Thây, as his students call him, has written many beautiful, clear, and simple books on meditation and has a special gift of teaching meditation to children.

The first step in this meditation is to go for a nature walk and collect ten pebbles. Look for pebbles that are especially beautiful to you, ones that "speak" to you or that you feel a special connection with. If possible, also find, or make, a nice little bag to keep your pebbles in when you are not using them for meditation.

To do this meditation, begin by sitting down, emptying your bag of pebbles, and putting all the pebbles on your right side. As you begin the pebble meditation, find the flow of your breathing, being mindful as you breathe in and out. As you breathe in, mindfully pick up one of the pebbles and hold it in your right hand. As you mindfully breathe out, pass the pebble from your right hand to your left hand with complete awareness, and set the pebble down on the floor next to you on your left side. With your next inhalation, pick up another pebble with your right hand, and continue as above, mindfully breathing, picking up, and passing the pebbles from the right to the left.

When you have mindfully transferred all ten pebbles from your right side to your left side, rejoice in having just performed a miracle of mindfulness. Then, if you have time, continue with this meditation, passing the stones one breath and one stone at a time, from your left back to your right. After ten mindful breaths, when you have moved each pebble from your left to your right, again rejoice in this marvelous feat, congratulate yourself! Reflect on what you have learned about making your mind and body one through mindful meditation, and generate a sincere wish to carry this mindful presence and careful attention into more activities of your daily life. Then mindfully pick up each pebble, one by one, thank them for helping you to develop your concentration and mindfulness, and put them back into the bag. Feel each one as you pick it up and let it go. Then close the bag and put it someplace where you will easily find it when you need it.

If you find it difficult to concentrate on the movements of the breath and the passing of the pebbles, experiment with synchronizing some simple phrases with your breathing and pebble passing. For example, as you breathe in and pick up a stone, say to yourself, "breathing in," and as you breathe out, pass the stone to your other hand, and set it down, say to yourself, "breathing out." You can also experiment with other phrases, such as "arriving . . . home . . . arriving . . . home," "receiving . . . releasing . . . receiving . . . releasing," or "here . . . now . . . here . . . now. . . ." If you prefer, make up phrases that you enjoy and that help you synchronize the activity of your body, speech, and mind all at the same time. What a miracle this is!

> *This pure Mind, which is the source of all things, shines forever with the radiance of its own perfection. But most people are not awar of it and think that the Mind is just the faculty that sees, hears, feels, and knows. Blinded by their own sight, hearing, feeling, and knowing they do not perceive the radiance of the Source.*
>
> *—Huang-po*

FIVE
REFLECTIVE MEDITATION

The unexamined life is not worth living.

—Socrates

THE INQUIRING MIND

"HOW DO YOU KNOW YOUR MOTHER is your mother?" No, this is not a Zen koan, this was Joel's first introduction to what is called analytical or reflective meditation. "It was my first day of high school," Joel recalls, "and my physics teacher, a brilliant scholar, social activist, and former Jesuit monk, gave us the following assignment: 'Write a paper showing me your reasoning and proofs for your assumption that your mother is truly your mother. What forces have shaped your thinking? What are you willing to question, and what are you afraid to question in your life? Search out and question your assumptions about reality. How do you really know what you believe is true? Where do you put your faith, and why?'"

You may be thinking to yourself, "Wait a minute—I thought meditation was about *stopping* my thoughts, not thinking. Do you mean to say that thinking can actually be a form of meditation? How can this be?"

To understand the answer to this question, can you remember a time when you were walking down the street or taking a shower and all of a sudden, out of the blue, you were struck by a brilliant idea, an inspiration for a project you were working on, an insight, or the answer to a question you may not even have known you were asking? Thinking is a natural display of the mind's radiant creativity. We all know how to think, but usually our thought process is lacking in coherence, focus, and depth. Consciously, and often unconsciously, the questions and yearnings in your mind seek for resolution and organize your thinking and attention to find the answer. From time to time, a stroke of genius will light up your mind with a brilliant insight, an "Aha!" that opens the way to a whole new understanding. To tap this creative power in a disciplined way is the practice of reflective meditation.

Once, in a conversation with the Dalai Lama, he pointed out that the main cause for the problems people in the West experience is the neglect of their inner life. The cure, he said, would come from people becoming more "inwardly aware" and, to some surprise, he said that introspection and reasoning would be a more efficient method to awaken this inner awareness than quiet meditation and prayer alone. Why? Because while quiet meditation and prayer may bring peace to the mind, they may not lead to the transformative insight and change of heart, the sense of certainty and faith, that can be awakened through more rigorous introspective or reflective styles of analytical meditation.

Reflective meditation is a domain of contemplative practice often overlooked, its significance neglected by many Western scholars, researchers, and critics of meditation. The transformative power of reflective meditation, however, is tremendous, and its methodology is both scientific and, in many ways, more familiar to most people than the quieter styles of meditation.

In reflective meditation, you select a theme, situation, or question as the focus of deep thinking, reasoning, and reflection. Properly directed, the flow of thought becomes more fluid, more coherent, and can lead to the emergence of qualities of mind that have great power and insight. After some time of analysis, this focused investigation culminates in the dawning of an insight, an "Aha!" or conclusion. When you reach a conclusion, your relationship to the idea or theme leaps to a different level. You now know it more intimately and relate to it with greater confidence, understanding its nature, value, and worth, appreciating its composition, essence, and reality more deeply.

In the next step of the reflective meditation process, you cease analyzing the subject and simply hold the theme unwaveringly in mind, allowing an even deeper quality of intuitive insight to emerge. This phase of the practice is actually a concentration meditation, taking the insight you have reached as your object.

Meditating on the insight in this way, the mind grows calm and clear. Its natural resonance seems to flow deep and strong without needing to precipitate cumbersome formulations of words. Quietly abiding in this calm yet energized state, the information of the insight is assimilated and integrated. If you maintain a steady, clear focus on your insight, it will deepen to reveal a deeper insight into the nature and reality of the theme of your reflection. When thoughts and associations begin to gather again within the mind, either conclude the session, carrying the uplifting inspiration of your insight with you, or enter into another, deeper cycle of reflective contemplation.

Alternating between periods of analysis and quiet intuitive introspection, layer upon layer of deeply seated and often erroneous "mental models," beliefs, and assumptions can be examined, questioned, and dismantled, revealing deeper and deeper levels of intuitive wisdom. Free from the clouds of confusion and the veils of ignorance, a lucid, bright faith may dawn in the clear sky of your mind.

Practiced in this way, reflective meditation awakens a wellspring of transformative power in the mind—the power to change the course of our lives. This power is drawn from the awakening of faith, born of reasoning and logic, which generates strong conviction and commitment and provides enormous leverage for making changes in our lives and world. It allows us to move mountains of the earth and the metaphorical mountains of our own looming and largely unquestioned assumptions. Such faith inspires our confidence and builds our trust. It gives us the strength to stay true to our most heartfelt aspirations and to what we know in our hearts to be true for us.

TRANSFORMING THOUGHT

Reality divided by reason always leaves a remainder.
After everything has been said about the universe, after
the entire world has been transformed on the basis of
scientific knowledge into a hierarchical structure of
|ever-widening systems, we are still invariably
left with a profound sense of mystery.

—Haridas Chaudhuri

Thoughts are the fossils of the living reality of life's experience. They freeze the flow of direct experience, shattering the stream into the illusion of an experiencer who stands apart from an experienced object. Understanding this dilemma, the contemplative traditions have developed many methods for enabling individuals to free themselves from confusion and illusion in order to encounter reality directly in its pristine nakedness.

Thoughts are thoughts. Stories are stories. And reality is reality. Reflective meditation helps us to recognize the ways we create and construct our world with our concepts. Most people live in an imaginary world, mistaking their beliefs, assumptions, fantasies, and thoughts for reality; adept meditators flirt with reality. Looking deeply into our mind, the structures of our thoughts are revealed, assumptions are questioned, and confusions and illusions are unraveled. Reflective meditation teaches us to appreciate the relativity of our thoughts and the stories that we tell ourselves. In the process we come to understand the difference between the reality of ourselves, others, and our world, and the stories that our thinking minds weave about those realities.

To mindfully recognize the reality of thoughts as expressions of a deeper reality of our being, to consciously engage in the thinking process in a more coherent and natural manner, and to maintain a presence of mind deeper than thoughts, is a fine art few people dream of mastering. When the nature of thought is properly understood, and when we learn to think deeply and clearly, thoughts are discovered to have a reality of their own, both different from and similar to what we had previously imagined.

Thoughts form the filters of our experience and are the lenses through which we view and experience the world. In the first stanza of the most widely quoted teaching of the *Dhammapada,* the Buddha says:

We are what we think.
All that we are arises with our thoughts.
With our thoughts we make the world.
Speak or act with an impure mind
And trouble will follow you
As the wheel follows the ox that draws the cart. . . .
Speak or act with a pure mind
And happiness will follow you
As your shadow, unshakable.

Chaotic thought leads to the experience of a chaotic world. As we bring greater coherence to our thinking, we behold a more coherent, orderly, and harmonious world. As a result, we feel as though we can relax. We no longer need to work so hard to make meaning out of the chaotic onslaught of discontinuities that characterize ordinary experience. Trusting the process, our need to assume a defensive attitude lessens and the mind naturally becomes quieter. With quiescence of mind comes a corresponding quieting of the brain-nervous system. New orders of coherence and harmony are allowed to emerge mentally, physically, spiritually, and in our deep relationship to the mysterious, many-dimensional universe in which we live.

THE POWER OF INSIGHT

Insight is the emergence within the mind of a meaningful pattern of relationship, indicative of deeper structures of the mind. It reflects subtler, higher-order patterns of mind intersecting with energy emerging and restructuring less subtle ones. The more profound the insight, the more transformative its power and the greater its capacity to restructure the subtle, responsive structures of the nervous system. As our thinking and reasoning become more coherent, inquiry culminates in the breakthrough of an insight that has a transformative effect upon us.

In moments of insight we participate in the emergence of deeper structures of mind and reality into conscious awareness. Many great mystics and scientists have regarded insight and inspiration as the infusion of supreme intelligence into our conscious minds. They describe how this infusion is capable of restructuring the matter of the brain that underlies thought, erasing patterns of the mind-brain that maintain the structure of our limiting, distorted, or confused storyline while leaving the brain-mind open to perceive reality in a different and deeper way. When these ordinary thinking structures are suspended, either spontaneously in times of danger, crisis, grace, or revelation, or through meditation, it is possible to glimpse a less filtered or even direct view of the way things really are. What is revealed is often so profound that a few timeless moments are sufficient to radically transform our orientation toward life. Like a small wingflap on a plane, even a small, but significant, shift in our attitude or orientation may be sufficient to completely change the course of our life and the ports of call that bless our path.

Most people unconsciously invest enormous amounts of energy and attention in organizing thought to maintain the illusion of their personal storyline. A meditator, however, is more likely to hold his or her story more lightly, appreciating its relatively true nature while staying open to the Mystery of wholeness that is always more vast and marvelous than our most creative imaginings. As the great Persian Sufi poet Rumi wrote, "When eventually you see through the veils to how things really are, you will keep saying again and again, 'This is certainly not like we thought it was!'"

THEMES FOR REFLECTIVE MEDITATION

A multitude of themes can be selected as the focus for your reflective meditations. Some classic themes include:

- Who am I?
- What is the meaning of life?
- What is the nature of change and impermanence?
- The preciousness of life and the inevitability and unpredictability of death.
- The presence of God's love in the world.
- The universal laws of cause and effect.
- The Stations of the Cross.

- The interdependence of all beings.
- Our place in the great chain of being—from our ancestors to generations to come.
- Who do I want to be when I grow up? *How* do I want to be when I grow up?
- What does E=MC^2 really mean?
- What legacy do I want to leave when I'm gone?
- What values and principles are worth living for?
- How can I help relieve the suffering of others?

Other traditional themes for reflection are a verse of scripture, a prayer, a sacred phrase, or a Zen koan such as, "What was my face before I was born?" "What is this?" or the classic (though often misquoted), "Two hands make a sound [Clap!]. What is the sound of one hand?"

In our daily life, reflective meditation can be applied to a host of projects, from designing a house to planning a presentation or searching for a breakthrough solution to a complex challenge. Some therapists use a form of guided reflective meditation to help clients better understand the workings of their minds and come to healing insights, or to help them awaken the confidence, faith, and commitment necessary to make needed changes in their lives. In our work as corporate consultants we often use types of reflective inquiry when we support R&D teams in developing new products, or others in finding creative solutions to challenges they are struggling with.

GUIDELINES FOR REFLECTIVE MEDITATION

The practice of reflective, or analytical, meditation can be outlined quite simply:

1. Select a theme or question about which to think deeply and wholeheartedly.

2. When your attention wanders, be vigilant enough to notice that it has wandered, and refocus on your selected theme or question. When the clarity of your attention fades, again be disciplined enough to notice that your attention is fading, heighten your clarity, and renew the contemplation of your chosen theme.

3. When you come to an insight or sense of "Aha!" allow the mind to simply rest in that state of openness and insight without analysis. Maintain a steady, clear focus on the insight and gently penetrate it more deeply to reveal even deeper levels of insight into the nature and reality of the theme for your contemplation.

4. When thoughts and associations begin to gather again within the mind, either conclude the session, carrying the upliftment of your insight with you, or enter into another cycle of reflective contemplation.

5. If you like, conclude your meditation by anchoring your insights through writing them down, creating a poem or affirmation, doodling an appropriate symbol, composing a dance, or playing a song that captures the spirit of your insight or revelation.

6. Remember, the deep mind will continue to search for inspirations and answers to your questions and prayers—even after you conclude your formal time of reflection. Stay mindful and open to the flow of insights, inspirations, and revelations that may emerge in quiet moments during the day or dance in your dreams at night.

While there are fewer meditations given below than in some other sections of this book, the introduction and guidelines above will help you apply these powerful principles to making reflective meditation a part of your life and work. Remember the words of the Buddha as you practice reflective meditation:

> Do not believe in what you have heard; do not believe in the traditions because they have been handed down for generations; do not believe in anything because it is rumored or spoken by many; do not believe merely because a written statement of some old sage is produced; do not believe in conjectures; do not believe in that as truth to which you have become attached by habit; do not believe merely the authority of your teachers and elders. After observation and analysis, when it agrees with reason and is conducive to the good and gain of one and all, then accept it, practice it, and live up to it.

SIX WAYS OF KNOWING:
A CURE FOR "PSYCHOSCLEROSIS"—
HARDENING OF THE ATTITUDES

In the Iroquois tradition, the elders of the tribe teach the young ones to look deeply into every situation and to come up with at least six levels of interpretation or explanation. So, pick a situation that challenges you to make sense of it. This may be a challenge that has developed at work or in a relationship, something related to the behavior or actions of another person, or this may be the reason that something happened or did not happen in your life.

Think deeply about the situation and come up with at least six different plausible explanations for it. Once each explanation is clear in your mind, assign a probability that reflects how likely that is the best explanation. Once you have ranked each explanation, mentally step back and contemplate the meaning-making workings of your mind and the relativity of every conclusion, interpretation, assumption, and belief that you may come to. Appreciate the power of such rigorous reasoning, and the wisdom to be found in uncertainty.

At first this may be a very difficult exercise for you, which may mean that you may have a serious case of "psychosclerosis"—hardening of the attitudes. Yet with practice, your thinking will grow more supple, your mind will open to recognize more possibilities, and this kind of reflective inquiry will become easier—and will be more fun to do.

CLEAR MIND, DON'T KNOW MIND

If your mind is empty, it is always ready for anything;
it is open to everything. In the beginner's mind there are
many possibilities; in the expert's mind there are few.

—*Shunryu Suzuki Roshi*

Living with an open mind and with questions offers far more possibilities than living with certainty and answers. The mind that knows it does not know is much more open to learning and discovery than the mind that thinks it has the answer.

An inspiring Korean Zen master we have studied with, Dae Soen Sa Nim, teaches a classical practice that opens the mind into the heart of awareness, challenging and inviting us to simultaneously hold knowing and not knowing, being in control and having faith to trust the flow. We often suggest this practice to people we work with to help them turn fixation into flow and to focus flow into clarity. This is how it works:

As you inhale, think or softly say to yourself:
"Clear mind, clear mind, clear mind . . ."
Then as you exhale, think or softly say:
"Don't knowwww . . . ."
Breathing in, "Clear mind, clear mind, clear mind . . ."
Breathing out, "Don't knowwww . . . ."
Continue . . .

Each inhalation focuses the mind, brings you to calm and clarity, gives you a firm, strong, sense of control, certainty, and a stable place to stand. And then—just let it all go, let it all flow, trust, step into the free fall and open to the Great Mystery that underlies everything we think we know for certain. With each breath there is both an invitation to focus and to flow. To take and then surrender control. With each breath, you focus, coalescing like a particle and expanding and opening into the mystery of your wave form nature. Each breath invites you to stretch between clear mind and don't know mind...certainty and uncertainty . . . particle and wave...clarity and trust...control and surrender. With each breath we learn to touch the earth, then the heavens. We learn to straddle the abyss of extremes and be wonder-struck by the wisdom revealed in paradox.

We know many people who use this method to help them focus, center, and find balance throughout the day. Some use it to clear their minds between meetings or sessions with clients, others to keep a light heart and open mind as they walk through crowded streets or sit in tense meetings. For others this centering technique is a focus for quiet contemplation. For many it has been the source of tremendous insight.

This method can have a very direct effect on putting things into perspective. It fiercely anchors and frees your attention by reminding you to find a balance between a clear mind and an open mind, and to welcome everything that comes to you with fresh, clear eyes and a deep bow of respect. Remember these words of Lao Tzu:

> In the pursuit of learning,
> every day something is acquired.
> In the pursuit of Tao,
> every day something is dropped.
> Less and less is done
> Until no-action is achieved.
> When nothing is done, nothing is left undone.
> The world is ruled by letting things take their course.
> It can not be ruled by interfering.

STANDING IN THE POSSIBILITY

> What vistas might we see if we were to understand
> the full power of the human mind? The human
> consciousness may prove the most inspiring frontier
> in our history, an endless wellspring of knowledge, and
> our means of liberation from all limitation....
> If we can find ways to awaken the full power of
> awareness, we could enter a new phase of human
> evolution and revitalize ourselves and our world.
>
> — *Tarthang Tulku*

As you begin this reflective meditation, mentally project yourself to a time five years into the future. Imagine yourself as you would most like to be, having accomplished the things you'd like to accomplish, learned what you would like to learn, and made the contributions you would like to have made.

Now consider:

What are the qualities you have developed in yourself?

What are the most important lessons you have learned?

What contributions do you feel most happy about having made?

In order to make these contributions, what strengths have you been willing to acknowledge in yourself?

In order to accomplish these things, what strengths have you learned to acknowledge in others?

Who or what have been the most important sources of inspiration and support for you?

What has provided the faith and courage to move forward at times when you felt stuck?

Now, standing in the present moment, consider what you can do right now in order to begin to accomplish these things and make these contributions.

If it feels right, make a commitment to yourself to take this vision to heart and make it a living reality.

TWO DOMAINS OF REALITY

*We are luminous beings. We are perceivers. We are
an awareness. We are not objects. We have no solidity.
We are boundless. The world of objects and solidity is a
way of making our passage on earth convenient. It is only
a description that was created to help us. We, or rather
our reasons, forget that the description is only a description and thus we entrap the totality of ourselves in
a vicious circle from which we rarely emerge in our
lifetime. . . . We are perceivers. The world that we
perceive is an illusion. It was created by a description
that was told to us since the moment we were born.*

—Don Juan

We live in a world with two domains of reality. There is the domain of conventional reality in which I am me and you are you, where this is a book, where objects have names and defined relationships. Then there is the domain of ultimate or absolute reality, the quantum soup, the field of undifferentiated morphic resonance, the domain of space-time and energy that is completely empty of isolated entities and which is the wholeness of all fields and continuums of interrelated energy and life.

Bringing an awareness of these two realities into our daily life can help us in so many ways. Certainly, we will develop more respect and a more sacred outlook toward the people and things that surround us. Numerous strategies can be used to cultivate this deep knowing into our lives. One Zen approach is to continually ask, "What is this?" When confronted with an object, a situation, don't attempt to analyze it, simply inquire, "What is this?" and let the mind gain direct insight into it by being completely open, receptive, alert, and investigative.

Another approach is to remind ourselves, "I'm only labeling this as . . . ." This helps to remind you that labeling or naming is simply the projection of a concept upon a field of phenomena. Understand the relativity and inadequacy of your imputations and mental projections. Open your mind to glimpse the nature of things unnamed and before thought, fresh, alive, and uncontrived.

Apply this same regard to yourself. As you investigate and reflect on "Who am I?" listen for answers that arise as the changing flow of physical sensations, emotional feelings, and states of mind or consciousness. Beware of any idea that you impute upon the totality of the process that is you. Experience and realize that you are far more than your thoughts of who you are. "Who are you . . . really?"

TRUE NATURE MEDITATION

When we look deeply into the heart of a flower,
we see clouds, sunshine, minerals, time, the earth,
and everything else in the cosmos in it. Without
clouds there could be no rain, and
without rain there would be no flower.

—Thich Nhat Hanh

Select an object: a flower, a piece of paper, an orange, or a person, and examine it carefully. As you direct your attention to this object, hold the question in mind, "What is this?" Notice all the thoughts and associations that arise in your mind in response to this question. Keep looking and thinking deeply into this object. If your mind wanders off to unrelated things, note the distraction, and return again to the object and the question, "What is this?" Let the many dimensions of this reality be revealed to you.

Thich Nhat Hanh sometimes teaches basic reflective meditation to children using a piece of paper. He will hold it up and ask them, "Do you know what this is?" And he invites the children into an inquiry to discover the "true nature" of the paper. "Oh yes, I can see the tree in the piece of paper!" "Can you see the clouds in the paper too?" "Can you see the sun, and the rain?" "Can you see the logging truck and the truck driver's mother?" "Can you see . . . ?" Upon careful examination, the whole universe is discovered by looking deeply into the fabric of the paper.

This is what Buddhists mean by "emptiness"—the paper is "empty" of being paper, because upon careful observation it is found to be full, or woven of, countless other things. Our previous assumptions, mental models, and prejudices about paper are radically restructured, leading us to a deeper sense of appreciation for all that a piece of paper really is. Along the way we will discover, question, and likely change some of our long-held and previously unexamined assumptions, beliefs, stereotypes, and mental models.

Each time we come to an insight, an "Aha!" that "changes our mind," there is also a restructuring of our reality—our sense of ourselves, our world, the structures and functions of our mind and brain. Eureka! The awakening of insight liberates us from confusion and allows the real world that was veiled by our thoughts to shine through more brightly and clearly in our minds.

WHO AM I?

We live in illusion and the appearance of things.
There is a Reality. You are that Reality. Seeing this,
you know that you are everything. And being
everything, you are nothing. That is all.

—*Kalu Rinpoche*

If you look deeply into yourself, can you find the mountain streams, the clouds, the sunshine, vineyards, orchards, and wheat fields within you? Looking at your hands or into the mirror, can you see your father and mother, your grandparents and ancestors? If you listen deeply to your "self-story," can you hear the whispers of wisdom and confusion, the love and the fear, the cruelty and the compassion of countless people, ancestors, and lifetimes?

If you ask me to point to "myself," that part of me that is most truly me, I'd have to laugh. It simply can't be done. "I" am this whole cast of characters, wise and woolly, loved and loathed, all the many voices that call themselves by my name. It is truly amazing how the myriad strong, compelling forces that drive our lives can be so invisible, ephemeral, so impossible to see or grasp. Still these intangible forces act so strongly on our lives, compelling us into actions even when we know they are not necessarily the most wise, kind, or balanced. To the degree that these forces are unknown or unowned by us, they are able to exert an often unbalancing influence over our life. And to the degree that we are mindful of these forces, we have more freedom, choice, and possibility in our lives.

As you begin to look deeply into your ordinary sense of self, it begins to unravel, revealing a deeper glimpse of your true and authentic self. Bernadette Roberts, a contemplative teacher who lived many years as a Catholic nun, explains that, "Emptiness is two things at once: the absence of self and the presence of the Divine. Thus as self decreases, the Divine increases." The great Taoist sage Tung Shan echoed this realization when he said,

> If you look for the truth outside yourself,
> it gets farther and farther away.
> Today, walking alone, I meet him everywhere I step.
> He is the same as me, yet I am not him.
> Only if you understand it in this way
> will you merge with the way things are.

THE PATH OF THE TWO SWORDS

Moment to moment you stand at a crossroads and life challenges you to choose a path. We are often mindless of the possibilities and choices, and the momentum of our unconscious habits makes the choice and runs our life for us. When no one is present, habit rules our life! In those moments we are awake, when we realize we do have a choice, the question is: Will you take a life-affirming step that feeds and nourishes your soul and affirms your authenticity and wholeness, or will you slip onto a path of fragmentation and inauthenticity that bleeds the vitality from your life?

In Japanese martial arts, this moment-to-moment challenge is represented in the tradition of the two swords. One is "the sword that gives life," katsujinken; the other is "the sword that takes life," satsujinoto. Moment to moment on your path of life you draw one of these swords. When you make a life-affirming choice or take a life-affirming action, you draw "the sword that gives life." When you act out of self-centeredness, mindless habit, fear, or reactivity, you draw "the sword that takes life," you bleed instead of feed yourself, depleting the vitality of your true spirit.

The great psychologist Abraham Maslow once said, "Think of life as a process of choices, one after another. At each point there is a progression choice and a regression choice. To make the growth choice instead of the fear choice a dozen times a day is to move a dozen times toward self-actualization."

Staying mindful of this moment-to-moment choice is an ongoing meditation practice. Some of our teachers have encouraged us to collect two bags of small pebbles—one bag of one color, black or green, and a bag of another color, white or brown, for example. At the end of each day reflect upon the moments you were mindful, present, kind, and made wise, life-affirming choices, and for each of these moments pull out and make a pile of stones from the first bag. Then, reflect upon all of the mindless, insincere, habit-driven, reactive, unkind moments of the day, the moments that depleted your vitality and aliveness. For each of these moments, pull out a pebble from the second bag and make a pile of these stones. Then sit and quietly reflect on how you lived today, what you learned, and how you aspire to live tomorrow.

With discipline and practice, we gradually increase our capacity to be fully present as we walk the path of life, and we will make more wise choices. A real master is not a person who is never distracted or wanders from the path; he or she is someone who is the quickest to recognize and correct their mistakes and to return to awareness when they have been momentarily distracted.

MEDITATION ON THE FIVE ELEMENTS

*When you walk across the fields with your
mind pure and holy, then from all the stones, and all
growing things, and all animals, the sparks of their
soul come out and cling to you, and then they
are purified and become a holy fire in you.*

—Hasidic saying

Begin this meditation with a few minutes of relaxation and breath awareness. Now bring your attention to the earth element of your body—that aspect of your existence which is dense and solid. Feel the massiveness of your body, its weight and form. As you breathe, contemplate and feel the element of earth experienced as form, density, mass, and weight.

Now shift your focus of attention to the water element—that aspect of your embodiment and of your world which is fluid and cohesive. Feel or imagine this dynamic fluidity as blood, lymph, and other waters of life flowing within your body. Sense and imagine this water element flowing through the world in which you live.

The element of fire is associated with the warmth, light, and heat of your body and of the world. Feel this inner heat, this vital warmth that dissipates at death. Experience how this element of heat and light is evident as it radiates in all living beings and through the world around you.

The air element is related to the spaces of the internal cavities, movement, and the flow of the breath. This function of respiration dynamically connects you to your world. At a more subtle level, this "air" element is associated with the movement of subtle energies throughout the body, sometimes pictured in acupuncture or esoteric anatomy charts. On a macro-scale, this element weaves the web of resonant energies which regulate the metabolism of the planet, and entrain and attune us with the movements of the heavens. Contemplate the pervasiveness of this air-wind element within and around you.

The faculty of awareness or knowingness is often associated with the most essential element. This most subtle element is not physical in nature. It is called by many names: "consciousness," "ether," "mind," "spirit," "that which does not die," etc. This is the animating force unique to life, the vital essence that sees through our eyes, listens through our ears, and is always awake in the heart of all living beings.

The contemplation of these five elements is used in many traditions as a means of enabling individuals to better align themselves with the inner and outer elements of life and the cosmos.

TRANSFORMING EMOTIONS

Ordinarily our emotional responses are highly conditioned and automatic. Blown by the winds of our emotions, we often experience confusion, disharmony, and physical disease. Once you understand this process, you can assume more control and responsibility for how you use your emotions. You can learn to regain your balance and bring harmony to your mindbody by generating appropriate emotions as an antidote to the self-centered and often destructive aspects of your emotional reactions.

In order to work on transforming our emotional reactions, it is necessary to first understand how emotions work. The Dalai Lama offers us some valuable insight when he teaches that, "Understanding a process enables a person to gain control of that process or to gain freedom from being controlled by it. Thus, analytic understanding of the atomic components of blind rage—what triggers it, how it directs itself, how it mobilizes mental, verbal, and physical energies and so on enables an habitually angry person to begin to control his or her temper, perhaps finally to become free of its control."

Remember, each emotion can be expressed from the true essence of the human spirit or from a distorted bias of our own self-centeredness. One will set you free, while the other will perpetually entrap you in a cycle of disharmony. For example:

Equanimity can lead to apathy;
Joyfulness to elation;
Compassion to sentimentality;
Love to attachment;

Meditation training helps you to focus your attention to understand the interplay of mental attitudes, emotional feelings, and physical reactions. As you come to understand this complex process, you can maintain or restore your internal balance by generating an emotion that is an appropriate antidote to a disturbing emotional state. For instance:

Love counteracts apathy;
Equanimity will ground you from elation;
Joyfulness will melt your fixation on sentimentality;
Compassion will inhibit attachment.

Some reflective meditations for understanding and transforming emotions include:

1. In an emotionally charged situation, focus your attention on the physical sensations in your body and on your own emotional feelings—not on the situation or on those involved. If you feel tension, holding, or squeezing in your body, bring your attention to those feelings. Breathe . . . and relax. Remember, you are the only one responsible for your mental, emotional, and physical response to the situation. Breathe, relax, and open your field of attention to find a creative solution or response to the challenge.

2. Investigate the physical sensations and mental images related to your emotional state. Reflect, "What does this fear, anger, sadness, or grief really feel like? Where do I feel it in my body? How big is it? Where does it come from or go to? What are the thoughts and mental tape-loops associated with this emotional state?" You will find that by simply investigating the nature of your emotional reactions, the intensity will diminish. You will be able to calm and clear your mind and to respond from a state of centered strength.

3. When you feel overwhelmed by other people's pain, let the pain break your heart open. Awaken genuine compassion: compassion for the difficulties and suffering or helplessness; compassion for your own

frustration or helplessness; compassion for all others who might feel as they or you feel in that situation.

4. When others act cruelly or insensitively, remember that no one can act that way unless they are suffering themselves. The more quickly you are able to recognize and transform your own negative emotional patterns, the less likely you are to hurt someone else.

5. Think about the irony of being angry about feeling angry, or guilty about feeling guilty. Learning to recognize and accept old conditioned emotional reactions is the first step to changing them.

6. Learn to befriend your confused or negative emotions. When a negative emotion arises, smile to yourself and mentally note, "Ah, anger (or blame, guilt, or jealousy) . . . of course!"

7. Develop flexibility of emotional response. In the face of anger, for example, practice generating compassion toward yourself and others. In the face of greed, practice generating gratitude for all that you have. When experiencing jealousy, try finding the feeling of rejoicing in the good fortune of another. When impatient, practice patience.

8. When all else fails, learn from your mistakes! Analyze the situation after it's over, clarify how you might improve your response in the future, and vividly imagine yourself in a similar situation responding the way you would like to.

As you develop the ability to authentically recognize and acknowledge what you are feeling, you will be better able to understand the destructive potential of negative emotional states. This direct understanding will enable you to consciously cultivate new and more effective emotional responses which bring greater balance and harmony to your mindbody, your behavior, and your relationships.

> *There comes a time in the spiritual journey when you start making choices from a very different place . . . . And if a choice lines up so that it supports truth, health, happiness, wisdom, and love, it's the right choice.*

> **—Angeles Arrien**

SIX
CREATIVE MEDITATION

The sense of wonder is based on the admission that our intellect is a limited and finite instrument of information and expression, reserved for specific practical uses, but not fit to represent the complete-ness of our being . . . . It is here that we come in direct touch with a reality which may baffle our intellect, but which fills us with that sense of wonder which opens the way to the inner sanctuary of the mind, to the heart of the great mystery of life and death, and beyond into the plenum void of inner space from which we derive our conception of an outer universe that we mistake for the only genuine reality. In other words, our reality is our own cre-ation, the creation of our senses as well as of our mind, and both depend on the level and the dimensions of our present state of consciousness.

—Lama Govinda

FOR THOSE OF US WHO HAVE a strong personal story line that runs, "I'm not creative," or for those who view imagination or visualization as unhealthy practices, the following "self-test" will help illuminate the innately creative nature of the mind. On a scale of 1 to 10—1 being "not at all" and 10 being "most of the time"—ask yourself the following questions:

- How good am I at worrying about things?
- How often do I notice judgments and projections in my mind about people—those I know, those I don't know, and even about myself?
- How vividly do I dream?
- How often do I notice that I am lost in my thoughts or daydreams?

If you know how to worry, pass judgment, project your fantasies about people you don't even know, or get lost in your thoughts, then congratulations—you have experience with the creative power of your mind.

The problem is that for most people creative intelligence is so unconscious, unproductive, or self-sabotaging that what comes up on the screen is a chaotic churn of mental cartoons that leave them feeling out of control and often frightened. "Worry is just misdirected prayer," says one of our Native American teachers. "It's like praying backwards!" The habits of the mind run deep, dampening our creativity and potential. It is estimated that the average person generates as many as 60,000 thoughts each day and that 90% of those thoughts are reruns—replays of thoughts we thought yesterday. Add to this the estimate that people spend an average 40% of their time worrying, and that 90% of what they worry about never comes true. Can you imagine how much more creative, healthy, productive, and happy you could be if you learned how to focus your naturally creative intelligence in a more conscious and productive way? This is what creative meditations are for.

Mindfulness practice gives us the skill, courage, and awareness to look deeply into this chaotic display; reflective and creative meditations transform wasteful habits of mind and channel the mind's creative energy with greater wisdom and compassion. Properly used, creative meditation helps us to harness and direct our intuition and our intention, or creative will.

Keep in mind that your motivation determines the effect of practicing any type of meditation. Some styles of meditation use methods of creative visualization to attract the perfect soulmate, become prosperous, or fulfill some other personal desire, but practicing meditation with self-centered motivation may only reinforce the illusion of a limited, separate self and, in the long run, actually impede spiritual growth. Though these practices may be used with either mundane or sublime motivations, meditation as a support for spiritual growth is always undertaken with an altruistic motivation. The ultimate expression of creative meditation is through prayer and creative compassion.

EXTRASENSORY IMAGINATION

Through creative meditation we attune and align ourselves with forces and realities in our lives we cannot sense with our ordinary senses. Fritjof Capra once said, "Physicists explore levels of matter; mystics explore levels of mind. What they have in common is that both levels lie beyond ordinary sense perception." Einstein came to the revelation of the famous $E=MC^2$ equation after envisioning himself traveling on a sunbeam at the speed of light. Discovered through a process of creative meditation, the profound meaning in this equation has radically transformed our world and humanity's vision of reality by showing the direct relationship between matter and energy.

Creative meditation provides us with tools to elaborate on cycles and relationships that we observe in nature by mentally extrapolating those harmonics of perception across time and space. Using a combination of inner and outer technology, we anticipate and calculate the times and size of tidal changes and predict precise times of lunar eclipses, meteor showers, or the returns of comets. Futurists, city planners, and marketing teams run mental simulations to identify the most probable conditions in the world to come, and then create plans to make those dreams a reality.

CREATIVE INTELLIGENCE

As we have seen in the last chapter, reflective meditation can reveal insights that help us to dismantle the cage of our misconceptions in order to see reality more clearly. It is in this light that creative meditation is best understood. Seeing the relativity of our mental projections, we learn to take them less seriously. This profound understanding helps us appreciate and liberate the radiant creative intelligence at the heart of all creation—and at the heart of our own deepest being.

Creative imagination and meditation invite our mind and heart to expand and invoke a broader spectrum of possibilities and potentials to come forth in our lives. The trick is to dance lightly with the illusions the mind conjures up, to hold them as "simulations" on your own personal "holodeck" and to use them to develop, affirm, and mature the most noble, wise, compassionate, and sacred attributes within yourself.

Through the practice of creative meditation, we ultimately come to realize that the creative impulse alive within us, properly understood, is the universal creative spirit. As our faith deepens, and we trust to let go of more of the fixations and limitations we have held to, this creative compassionate intelligence comes more and more alive in and through our lives. My will becomes "Thy will," my love "Thy Love," my presence "Thy Presence."

CREATIVE IMAGINATION

Imagery and creative visualization are universal mental functions common to every human being. Though they play a critical role in our psychological and physical health, performance, and creativity, these capabilities are poorly understood and are seldom developed to their full potential. By bringing these ordinarily unconscious mental processes into conscious awareness, we can learn to dramatically expand the scope of possibilities available to us.

It is helpful to distinguish between spontaneous mental imagery and creative visualization. Imagery rich in information is continually arising within the mind—fantasies of the future, memories of the past, dreams, visions, our own self-image, and myriad expectations we project upon our world. Properly understood, imagery is the stuff of revelation and intuition. Within the gestalt of a single mental image is encoded information which, when spun into concepts, words, or mathematical or musical formulas, could fill many volumes. Some mental images are experienced consciously; others are edited out by our belief system or are simply too subtle to be recognized.

Mindfulness of spontaneously arising mental imagery serves primarily a "read-out" function. Creative imagination and visualization are more active functions of the mind. With visualization we are intentionally involved in generating and shaping the stream of mind-energy into prescribed mental images. Visualization equips us with a powerful tool for mentally simulating complex processes or possible futures beyond the scope of ordinary perception and thinking. "Imagination is more important than knowledge," said

Einstein, who understood well the interdependence of creative vision and intuitive wisdom.

Understanding that every mental image directly influences our body, new dimensions of self-mastery or self-sabotage become clear to us. Although an actual or anticipated experience may last only a minute, our innate imaginative capacity to remember or anticipate the experience may trigger similar mental, emotional, and physiological reactions again and again. Bringing these emotionally charged images to conscious awareness, we can then learn to creatively and productively control our imagination, and not only master the psychosomatic symptoms associated with distress and anxiety, but also energize and strengthen positive, healing qualities of mind. Learning the inner language of "listening" to spontaneous imagery and "speaking" with creative visualization, we equip ourselves with critical skills for optimizing many of the functions of our mindbody and realizing extraordinary levels of health and performance.

For example, if we imagine that we are feeling the warm rays of the sun, this may trigger a response that dilates our blood vessels, warms our hands, and lowers our blood pressure. Images of aggression can lead to the secretion of neurotransmitters associated with anger or fear, increasing heart rate, muscle tension, and blood pressure. Similarly, the image of biting into a tart, juicy grapefruit can cause saliva to flow; the memory of a tender embrace may fill us with the pleasant tingles of sexual arousal. When tested, athletes who mentally simulated shooting baskets each day out-performed others who had actually practiced for the same length of time on the court.

By calling forth a memory of a peak experience, we can awaken in the present moment those life-giving forces and character strengths that inspired past performance. Remembering the example of an inspiring teacher or role model or visualizing their presence can enable us to align our own thinking, will, and behavior with theirs.

TRADITIONAL CREATIVE MEDITATIONS

In the world's great spiritual traditions, creative meditations have been used in numerous ways. Here are some classic examples:

- Creative meditations are universally used for self-healing and in healing prayer.

- The simplest blessing, if taken to heart, invokes a brief but potent creative meditation for the mind. In the Jewish tradition there is a blessing or *brakha* for virtually every action taken in daily life. These brief prayers transform ordinary action into a *mitzvah*—which fulfills the commandments to live a holy life. Waking up, washing your hands, putting on your clothes, are all transformed into mini-celebrations of thanksgiving. In the Vietnamese Buddhist tradition, the short meditational prayers, or *gathas,* are frequently used in a similar way to transform ordinary action and perception into a path of awakening and enlightenment. An example of a gatha is: "Listen, listen, this wonderful sound brings me back to my true self."

(It is important to remember that creative meditations work through all the senses and doors of perception—auditory, kinesthetic, etc.—and are not limited solely to visual images, even though we commonly use the term "visualization" to include all kinds of mental images.)

- In a similar way, the invocations, visualizations, prayers, and affirmations of a priest and congregation celebrating the Eucharist in the Catholic Mass transform ordinary bread and wine into the sacred body and blood of Christ.

๑ Comparable practices found in all the world's great mystical traditions are used to purify and transform ordinary substances into potentized sacraments and medicines. One healing technique common to many traditions is to transform ordinary water into a healing elixir through prayer and meditation. During a lecture we presented at a national pharmacists' convention, a number of attendees spoke of how they would pray and bless medications before giving them to their clients. The effects of such creative meditations have been scientifically measured and confirmed in dozens of experiments!

๑ In the Tibetan Vajrayana tradition, reflective meditation is used first to identify and deconstruct the fixations and distortions that configure our ordinary sense of self. Having come to the realization that our ordinary "self" is largely a fantasy anyway, creative meditation is then used to generate, reconstruct, and embody the self in a way that is more aligned with our true, universal, and divine nature, rooted in wholeness inseparable from all of creation. These creative meditations not only generate cosmic dimensions of our appearance but also affirm the "sacred dignity" of our divine identity and our compassionate activity as radiant beings actively engaged in transforming the suffering of the world, and awakening all beings to their true nature and potential.

๑ Creative meditation, movement, and breathing exercises are used throughout Eastern and Western contemplative traditions, as well as in the martial arts and indigenous healing traditions of the world, to purify, balance, and "rewire" the subtle structures and substances of the inner energy system, regarded as the formative matrix from which our ordinary dense material body arises.

෧ In Sufi *tassawari* practices, meditators attune themselves to the spirit of various masters, saints, or prophets by reciting their sacred names and embodying their qualities. Sufis practice doing the "walk of Jesus," the "walk of Mohammed," the "walk of Mary," or invoke the presence of an archangel to "walk with" in order to bring alive within themselves the energy and embodiment of these great beings. Similar creative meditation practices are also used to attune to the subtle qualities associated with the different planets in our solar system.

෧ In many traditions, mandalas, medicine wheels, sand paintings, and sacred circles are visualized or created to aid meditators in transforming their vision of the world into a sacred world radiant in powerful blessings.

DEVELOPING YOUR CREATIVE IMAGINATION

The following strategies will help you discover and develop the creative visualization and imagination skills that work best for you.

1. Projective and Associative Imagination
   There are two approaches to visualization: projective and associative. Using projective visualization, you assume the view of an observer of the action—

you see yourself giving a dynamic presentation or skiing down a slope in deep powder snow. With an associative approach, you identify with the action and embody the experience—looking out through your mind's eye you behold the keen interest in the eyes of your listeners, or feel the spray of the snow in your face, and sense an exhilarating thrill of aliveness. Each of these exercises can be "viewed" from the detached, objective stance of an outside observer, or as a vivid, virtual reality of affirmed, embodied experience. Experiment and discover what works best for you.

2. Remember, Imagination and Visualization Are Not Always Visual

Can you imagine hearing the tune of *Jingle Bells*? How about smelling the smoke and feeling the warmth of a campfire? Can you imagine feeling the tender caress and savoring the scent of someone you love? Creative imagination works best when you involve all of your senses to create a multi-sensory gestalt of synesthetic experience.

3. The Kinesthetic, Dimensional, and Dynamic Approach

In the space before you, visualize an object. Imagine what it would be like to reach out and touch that object. If you are visualizing an apple, reach out and hold it in your hand. Allow it to become "real" for you as you sense its shape, weight, and size. Imagine holding the hand of a loved one, sense its warmth and aliveness. Envision yourself flowing through a sequence of movements to accomplish a task, feel your body moving, carving out space with patterns of motion. Infuse your visualizations with a dynamic, radiant sense of energy and aliveness.

4. Affirming the Image
Whether or not you can actually see or feel the visualized object or experience, mentally affirm that it is indeed there. This is like waking up one morning to find your surroundings shrouded in thick fog. Although you cannot see clearly the nearby house and trees, you still know they are there. If you are imagining an internal feeling, mentally and emotionally affirm that it is indeed a living reality within you, only at a level of sensitivity below the threshold of your awareness. With practice, build the vividness of these qualities until you are confident they are radiantly alive within you.

5. Fill in the Details or Begin with a Fragment
You may find it helpful to begin with a sense of the outline of an object and then fill in the details. For example, when visualizing a person, begin by envisioning their shape or form and then mentally add the details as clearly as possible. Similarly, experiment with beginning with a tiny piece of the image and then mentally develop it. Start by imagining a person's smile, then mentally paint in the rest of their face and body. Along the way if portions seem to fade out or dissolve, gently focus the flow of imagery to bring those regions back into view.

6. Affirm the Completeness of the Image or Process
Although the total image or scenario may not appear to you clearly, affirm its completeness. If, for example, you are visualizing a healing process, imagine that it has already worked through to completion. See, feel, and affirm yourself as healed and

whole. Envision standing in the possibility as though it were an actual reality.

7. Objectless Imagery

Some of the most powerful types of visualization for enhancing health, performance, and understanding of the mind involve objectless imagery of volume, distance, and spatial relationships. Is it possible for you to imagine the volume of your hands . . . or of your whole body? Sense the space and distance between you and the objects or people that surround you. Can you imagine hearing the silence before, between, and after sounds . . . or discover the space between the thoughts and the images floating through your mind? As you become more intimately aware of space as a medium of relationship, connectedness, and communication, you discover that space connects everything—separateness is a mere optical delusion of consciousness.

8. Morph and Multiply the Image

Once you begin to develop your "mental simulation" ability, expand your capacity by making imagined objects bigger or smaller, by "morphing" the image into something else, or by multiplying the image so that one becomes many, or many become one. When you have learned to do this in your waking life, look for opportunities to stretch these imaginative skills in your dreams and see what happens.

By becoming mindful of the dynamic, fluid, and insubstantial nature of mental images, you will be better prepared to work wisely with creative visualization. This insight into the fluid nature of mind-stuff is of critical importance. Without this recognition, there is the danger of using visualization to further deepen the illusion of substantiality and solidity, rather than to awaken greater wisdom, compassion, and freedom. Recognizing the dreamlike insubstantiality of the flow of images in the mind, and considering how compelled most people are by these largely unconscious images, a genuine sense of compassion may well up within you. Bringing the image-generating process of the mind into the domain of conscious awareness, compulsive reactivity will diminish and wisdom and freedom will grow. You will discover more creative options and make wiser decisions. Integrating these skills and insights, you will be well equipped to wisely use and apply creative meditation skills to enhance the quality of life—your own and others.

The creative meditations that follow reflect many different styles of practice. Approach them with curiosity and experiment. Let them stretch your sense of who you are and what is possible, and awaken within you a yearning to discover who you really are!

CONTINUUM

As you breathe, draw your awareness into this moment.

Exhaling, allow your awareness to flow effortlessly into the next moment. As you inhale, stabilize and focus your awareness into this moment. Exhaling, feel the flow of your being unfolding, moving, and continuously expressing itself through the medium of time and space.

Standing in the present, step into the future and leave the past irretrievably behind you. As you move, feel yourself emanating and moving forward through space and time.

Imagine that as you move you trace a pathway of light and energy through the fabric of space and time. Imagine that if you turned around you could actually see this luminous path, like a firefly in the night.

Now, imagine the path you have traced through the world today, during the past week, the last month. Sense the patterns, cycles, and rhythms of your goings and comings.

Imagine arising and retracing your steps as you moved around the house, drove to work or school, dropped into your favorite stores, visited friends, went for walks or bike rides. See your life as a continuum of light-energy patterns unfolding through space and time.

Imagine the pattern of your continuum unfolding since you were born. Even try to imagine the energy patterns of the body you were in before this one, and the one before that, and so on, back and back. Really feel yourself as a dynamic process expressing and unfolding itself through space and time.

Imagine the tons of universe that have sustained you and that you have burned as air and water and food during your life's—your *lives'*—journey.

Imagine moments of being in love, experiences of joy, of anger. Feel how your energy pervades space and affects the people all around you.

See how a simple apple is a continuum, a fusion of sunlight, water, earth, air, and the trees and apples that came before it. Imagine the kindness and work of the many people and creatures who have caused you to finally have this apple. Where does this apple-energy begin or end? Where does your field of energy begin or end?

Imagine your friends and companions. See them as merely a perceptual snapshot of a continuum of being. See the forest, flowers, objects as simply a process. Trace your tie pin, the cotton in your blouse, back to their organic roots in the earth. See everything as interwoven pathways of light and energy unfolding through space and time. People, planets, galaxies, atomic clouds of energy, whirling, unfolding beginninglessly and endlessly through time and space.

Thoughts, dreams, fantasies, and memories—all the play and processes of your mind.

Exhaling, imagine releasing some old grudge or limitation. Inhaling, receive new strength, wisdom, and energy. Use your cycles of breath to let go of old limiting postures, attitudes, and emotions that keep you from moving freely through life. With each breath, receive inspiration to nurture those qualities you wish to strengthen.

Life is made of moments. What ripens in any moment are seeds sown in the past. In this moment we can consciously sow seeds for happiness and health in the future.

Breathe your awareness into this moment.

As you exhale, allow your continuum to unfold with peace, balance, and joy.

THE ELEMENTAL BREATHS

The following series of Elemental Purification Breaths come to us through one of the lineages of Sufi teachings. This is a perfect focusing and centering practice to begin your day, and takes only the time of twenty-five breaths. It can be used as a short and simple meditation practice in itself, or as a warm-up concentration exercise to focus the mind for another meditation practice you may choose to do.

If possible, it is recommended to do this practice barefoot in the dewy grass at dawn as you watch the rising sun. The world is charged then with energy and potential, and within your own body, heart, and soul, this vitality and potential is reflected. If you are drawn to do this meditation at other times or in other places, that will be fine also.

First, with a series of five breaths, purify yourself with the energy and magnetism of the earth element, breathing naturally in and out through your nostrils. As you inhale, imagine that you draw the energy and magnetism of the earth up into you. It circulates through your subtle energy systems and replenishes and renews the magnetism of your body. As you exhale, imagine that the magnetic field of the earth draws all the heavy, gross elements or energies within you down into the ground to be purified and released. With each breath you feel revitalized, lighter, less dense, and more clear to the free flow of breath, life, energy.

Then with a second series of five breaths, imagine purifying yourself with the energy of water. Inhaling through your nose and exhaling through your mouth, envision a waterfall of pure, clear energy pouring down into you from the heavens above, flowing through you, and dissolving, purifying anything within you that might block the flow of life-energy moving through you. With each breath you are washed clean and clear as this stream of energy and light flows through you.

With the next series of five breaths, purify yourself with the element of fire. Inhaling through your mouth and exhaling through your nostrils, let the breath flow focus at your solar plexus as you inhale, and then rise up and radiate as light from your heart-center, shining out between your shoulder blades, and like a fountain of light up through the crown of your head. Inhaling fire, exhaling light, envision and affirm that this circulation of energy is a purifying fire gathering any remaining impurities or congestion and burning them into radiance and light in the fires of your heart.

With the next cycle of breaths, imagine purifying yourself with the air element. Inhaling and exhaling through your mouth, imagine the air element sweeping through you like the wind blowing through the spaces of your whole body, purifying any sense of density or obstruction that may remain.

Finally, breathing very gently through your nostrils for the last series of five breaths, envision yourself being purified by the most subtle element—the "ether" element of the ancients, or the most subtle energies that infuse space, or the quantum field of infinite potentials. Let this most subtle breath dissolve any remaining sense of solidity or density, and let your heart and mind open to be clear and vast like the infinite sky.

Energized and purified, sense the subtle, potentially profound shift that has taken place in the course of only twenty-five breaths. Carry the sense of calm and deep connectedness from this practice into your next meditation or into your daily life.

THE CIRCLE BREATH

In this exercise, we'll introduce you to another extremely useful meditation for balancing and focusing the energies of your mindbody. We use this technique often when we're walking or sitting quietly.

Once again, begin by becoming aware of your body and the natural flow of your breathing. As you inhale, bring your attention to the center of your body, just below the navel, and then allow your attention to move up along the back of your body to the top of your head.

As you exhale, imagine your breath circling down along and over the front of your body to your navel.

Inhaling, again draw your awareness from your navel up along your back to your crown; exhaling, move it down along the front of your body to your navel.

The flow of the breath defines a circle rising up the back and then flowing down the front of the body. The beginning and end point of the breath is at or just below the navel, at the center of your body. At the peak of your inhalation, your attention is focused at the top of your head for a moment.

Practice until you establish an easy, effortless, circular flow of energy around this orbit. Once you know how to initiate this flow of balancing energy and awareness, you will be able to rest in this circulation of energy while engaged in other activities.

This practice may at first feel awkward, but as with all learning, when you become more familiar with organizing your energy and awareness in this new way, it will begin to feel more natural and unfold in effortless and deeply sensed ways.

This is an excellent practice to stay centered and grounded amid the turbulence and distraction of your daily life. As with so many of the other meditation practices, the more you do this, the easier it will be to activate it when you need it.

HOLLOW BODY MEDITATION

One of the most effective techniques for dissipating accumulated stress and tension is to experience your body as hollow, open, and filled with clear space. Experience this space as neither solid nor empty, but rather as an inner openness within which feelings and sensations can freely come and go. This inner openness and spaciousness is devoid of any obstruction or any sense of solidity and denseness.

This deceptively simple method has been used for thousands of years and has recently been extensively documented to promote the integration and optimization of neuro-muscular, autonomic, and central nervous system functions, as well as to reduce pain and enhance endurance and overall mind-body coordination.

Begin by sitting comfortably with your spine straight and your body relaxed. Now, bring your attention to your breath, and as you inhale imagine drawing your attention into your head. It may be helpful to imagine the breath like a luminous crystal mist that completely fills your head. As you breathe out, let go of the image or feeling of denseness or solidity and imagine this region as completely open and filled with space. Sense and feel the sensations and vibrations that come and flow freely within this open space inside your head. With your next breath, draw your attention into your neck and throat, filling this region similarly with a sense of space—open to the flow of life energy, vibration, and sensation.

Continue now to breathe your awareness region by region into each part of your body. One region at a time, breathe this sense of luminous open space into your hands, arms and shoulders, your chest, abdomen, hips and buttocks and genitals, and finally your legs and feet. As you exhale, feel and vividly imagine that each region is left feeling utterly open to the flowing streams of sensation and vibration that knit the fabric of your experience. Amidst this flow of vibration and sensation, experience the inner quiet stillness and peacefulness that accommodate all these myriad changes and vibrations.

Now simply rest in this experience of your hollow body without conceptualization or analysis. Simply allow thoughts, feelings, perceptions, and images to arise and dissolve like luminous bubbles and streams flowing within this inner space of awareness. Experience your body as unified and whole, completely open to equalizing and diffusing the accumulated pressures of your body and mind. Allow each breath to deepen this inner harmony and to energize the calm intensity of your awareness.

Initially you may find that some regions feel dense, solid, and impregnable. You may be unable to get a clear feeling for these regions. Many people have cut themselves off from parts of their body due to past injuries, surgery, abuse as a child, or other conscious or suppressed trauma. So long as there are parts of your body cut off from your sense of wholeness, parts of your brain and mind potentials are blocked as well. These "locked closets" of your body leave you vulnerable as they are often the breeding ground for degenerative disease and cancer. In this case, combine your practice of this technique with Mindfulness of Your Body: Mental Massage (page 88).

Gradually, you will easily be able to imagine and actually feel that your whole body, from the top of your head to the tip of your toes, is completely open, unobstructed, unified, and radiant. This inner sense of your wholeness will enable you to reclaim those lost regions of your body, brain, and mind. Eventually you will be able to access this unified, open and luminous sense of your entire body with a single breath.

The following variations on the hollow body technique will further enhance your mind-body coordination and self-healing abilities.

1. Having dissolved your whole body into a unified sphere of empty openness, imagine your body in different sizes. Gradually allow your sense of your body to grow smaller and smaller. Reduce it to the size of a sesame seed and then expand it until it contains the room, the building, the globe, the Milky Way, and the universe. Take as much time as you need to vividly sense and flex these undeveloped capacities of your mind. Alternate between tiny and vast as you feel comfortable, maintaining a feeling of hollowness and luminous openness throughout.

2. Allow your body to appear and feel hollow and radiant, and expand this awareness to fill the universe. Then gradually imagine the entire universe dissolving down to absorb into your body. Next,

imagine your body dissolving from top and bottom into a small sphere of light at the center of your chest. Imagine this tiny luminous sphere growing smaller and smaller until your mind simply dissolves into a state of lucid openness.

Now rest in this state of clarity and openness. As the first thought arises in the stillness of your mind, immediately generate yourself as your hollow body again, yet this time feel as though all of your old limiting thoughts, negative habits of perception and behavior, and physical congestions have completely dissolved into space and that you are arising fresh, clean, clear, radiant, and purified—in a sense reborn.

As you move throughout your day, carry this inner sense of unified openness and wholeness with you. Frequently use the breath to help you renew this awareness. To deepen and enhance the benefits of this technique, train your mind to pay attention to the space and distance between things, and to imagine and sense the volume and natural radiance of other people and objects. Notice how the spaces between buildings, cars, people, and clouds actually connect everything. Train your inner and outer perception to experience how space, within and without, connects everything. With practice you will learn to recognize space as a unifying medium rich in information of many frequencies and wavelengths transduced by our ordinary and subtle senses. This quality of sensitivity can be enhanced further by practicing listening for the silences between sounds, and noticing the space between thoughts. This is a necessary foundation for cultivating your intuition and expanding the range of your subtle senses. With frequent practice of these techniques, the strength of old limiting patterns will gradually diminish, allowing you to access more effective and creative responses to the opportunities and challenges of your life.

HEAVEN AND EARTH SPIRALS

When you make the two one,
and when you make the inner as the outer
and the outer as the inner
and the above as the below,
and when you make the male
and female into a single one—
then shall you enter the Kingdom.

—Jesus in the Gospel of Saint Thomas

In one way or the other, many of our teachers have said that your ability to reach to the heavens is dependent on how deep your roots are in the mud of the earth. One especially powerful method of staying present, balanced, and centered throughout the day is to experience yourself as a conduit for the flowing energies of the earth and heavens. Since the electrical conductance at your feet and at your head have inverse properties, there's actually a basis in the body's bioelectrodynamics to support this practice. The universality of this method is reflected in the fact that variations of it have been used in many cultures around the globe for thousands of years. This is how it goes:

1. As you sit or stand quietly, sense or vividly imagine a dynamic powerful spiral of energy rising from the earth up through your body and then opening into the sky. Just be with this image or this sense for a few moments, allowing it to emerge as naturally as possible into your awareness. Breathing in, draw

the energy of the earth up and into you. Exhaling, feel this flow of energy rising up through your body and opening upward into the sky, drawing the energy of the earth up and into yourself, and then offering it upward and into the sky. As you begin to do this, you may find it helpful to use one of your hands to make an uplifting spiral, reaching up from the earth and spiraling up to the heavens.

As you breathe and continue this image, try to imagine this rising vortex of energy spiraling through you with a deep and powerful cleansing action. This dust-busting vortex dissolves any blockages to the free flow of the energy of your whole mindbody and leaves you feeling clean and clear, as though your energy and vibration of your life-force have bumped up a notch, leaving you feeling vitalized and keenly aware.

Keep in mind that if this kind of visualization exercise is difficult for you, just relax and give it your best. It's important to remember that, as with most of these exercises, you'll find the more effortlessly you hold the image and allow it to happen, the more vividly you'll be able to actually experience its reality.

2. As you breathe, this time simply allow the flow of earth energy to continue to rise and flow in the background. Now, focus your attention so that as you inhale you imagine drawing a vortex of energy or light down into you from the heavens above. Use all the special effects you can to make the visualization as vivid or as deeply felt as possible. Can you now imagine that you fill yourself with the energy of the heavens, and that as you exhale, it spirals down and through you into the earth? Drawing in

the heavens, bring that energy or light down through you into the earth like a wave of blessings. Let this shower of light and energy wash through you, cleaning and clearing your body and mind of any energies that get in the way of the flow. Feel your body and mind sparkling clean and clear in this balancing flow. Let the descending wave smooth, balance and ground your energy, and deepen your sense of stability and rootedness in the earth.

3. Once you have established the ascending and descending flows of energy, simply rest in the flow of awareness of both of these two spirals flowing through you at the same time. As these streams of light meet at the center of your heart, let them open your heart and mind to a state of natural radiance. Sense or imagine that as you rest within the flow of this dual stream, any energy that's blocked or frozen within you simply dissolves and melts into the flow. Allow any sense of denseness or solidity in your mindbody to dissolve and find its dynamic balance as a higher order of stability and strength that is pure, flowing energy and light.

Though at first you may just get the idea of what this image suggests, with practice this will become a very real and powerful experience for you. Be patient, don't expect fireworks or anything special. Just let your mind move like a magnet over a jumbled pile of iron filings and know that as your mind moves, all of the energies and particles within you will begin to align. Allow the energy that's already here within you begin to flow more smoothly.

As with many of the methods you're learning, the actual form of this meditation is very simple, yet the power and insight this practice can generate over time can be quite profound. Throughout the day, if it feels right to you, when you're sitting at your desk, on the bus, or walking down the street, activate your awareness of these spirals of energy and light flooding through you. As you do, awaken to and rejoice in your groundedness and connectedness to the strength, steadiness, and nurturing nature of the earth, and to the open, light, majesty, mystery, and vast potential of the heavens. Realize that though you may not be aware of them, you're never separate from these realities even for an instant. Practicing in this way will quietly, powerfully, and invisibly equip you with a way of moving through the world in balance, leaving a trail of light, good vibes and blessings wherever you go.

SLEEPING MEDITATION

Once upon a time, I, Chuang Tzu, dreamt I was a butterfly, fluttering hither and thither, to all intents and purposes a butterfly. I was conscious only of following my fancies as a butterfly, and was unconscious of my individuality as a man. Suddenly I awakened, and there I lay, myself again. Now I do not know whether I was then a man dreaming I was a butterfly, or whether I am now a butterfly dreaming I am a man.

—Chuang Tzu

There are numerous approaches to sleeping meditatively. One method is to simply meditate and relax before you go to bed. Take a few minutes to center and calm your mind, then review the day. Appreciate your day and as you notice moments about which you might feel some regret, appreciate the positive lessons these mistakes may hold for your actions in the days to come. In your heart say "thank you" to everyone who contributed to your learning and growth today. In your heart, give and ask forgiveness where needed, and feel as though you can sleep in peace. For optimum "recharging" of your energy system as you rest, many traditions recommend you sleep with your head to the north— to be in alignment with the electromagnetic field of the earth—and that you lie on your right side to minimize pressure on your heart, freeing up the circulation so the heart doesn't have to pump as hard.

Another technique for sleeping is to imagine that your bed is within a large luminous lotus bud or a small temple with a healing and regenerating light that infuses you as you sleep. Imagine that the resonance and light of this space surrounds you with a buffer zone against any harsh interference from the outer world. Imagine that it draws into itself all of the positive energy of the universe that may be helpful for you. Rest deeply, and upon awakening simply dissolve this visualization into rainbow light and absorb its essence into you.

Another method is to imagine that as you sleep you rest your head in the lap of a special teacher or protector who watches over you. Let all of your thoughts and cares be dissolved by their presence. Receive their love, strength, and inspiration as you sleep. Upon awakening, dissolve them into rainbow light and melt them into space, or into your heart. This technique can be combined with the previous method.

Yet another technique: as you lie in bed, imagine that with each breath you become filled with more and more light and space. As you exhale, you and everything in the universe melt into an ocean of light and space. Let your mind completely open like a drop falling into a luminous ocean. Rest deeply and powerfully. Upon awakening, let body and world appear fresh and new.

ARCHANGEL MEDITATION

A Hebrew invocation of the four archangels, from one of our teachers, Rabbi Shlomo Carlebach, has inspired the following meditation. This one is especially wonderful to do at bedtime.

As you prepare to go to sleep, invite holy angelic presences to surround you with heavenly protection throughout the night. Visualize, in the space above you on the right side of your bed, the presence of the archangel Michael, angel of mercy and loving-kindness. In Hebrew, Michael's name means "who is like God." At your left side stands the archangel of divine strength and courage, Gabriel. In front of you is Uriel, angelic messenger of divine light and clear vision. And directly behind you is the archangel of healing, Raphael. In the center of the four directions, shining down above your head, is the Holy Presence of Shekhinat El, the divine feminine aspect of God, whose name in Hebrew means "She Who Dwells Within."

If you do this meditation in the traditional way, facing east, then the four guardian archangels form a medicine-wheel mandala with Michael in the south, Gabriel in the north, Uriel in the east, and Raphael in the west. The Shekhinah remains unwaveringly always in the center, above you and within you.

This sleeping meditation can also inspire a creative daily meditation as well. Carrying the awareness of these heavenly guardian messengers with you throughout the day, whenever you have the need for greater clarity or vision (Uriel); for loving-kindness, mercy, and compassion (Michael); to summon more courage and strength (Gabriel); or to activate powers of healing (Raphael); simply turn and face the direction of the archangel whose energies and support you are calling for and invite their holy presence into your awareness. It is not necessary to actually physically turn and change direction if this is not possible or appropriate at the moment. Since these beings of light are of the nature of wisdom and compassion, just invoking them from your heart and asking for their presence by your side, in front, behind you, or above you, is all you need to do for it to be so.

DREAM YOGA: THE PRACTICE OF WAKING UP

Many people say their lives are so busy that they don't have time for meditation. Yet every living being must sleep. During sleep time, we don't schedule meetings or have appointments to keep. The time is ours, and is usually subject to the mindless, random chaos of our undisciplined minds. We spend nearly one-third of our life sleeping and dreaming. That means that if we live to be ninety, we would have spent thirty years of our life asleep. Can you imagine what it would mean if you were able to understand what is going on during those lost years of your life and to tap that mental power and creativity as a source of spiritual awakening?

In many of the great wisdom traditions of the world, there are traditions of "dream yoga" meditations that cultivate a sense of lucid wakefulness within the dream state. The profound practices of dream yoga blend the lucid clarity of mindful presence with the boundless creativity of the mind. And they combine elements of creative, reflective, and receptive meditation practices. Before you go to sleep, hold the clear intention to wake up and be conscious within your dreams. In some Native American traditions, dreamers are advised to remember to look at their hands within a dream, or to raise their hands to the sky in a prayer for rain to bless the earth. Holding a simple intent like this is a good place to begin a dream yoga practice.

Dreams have much to teach us about how we "construct" our experiences and sense of identity or self in our waking life. During mindless daily life, we seldom look deeply enough into our perceptions, conceptions, and projections to recognize that our selective attention, biases, preconceptions, and assumptions are actually weaving together to construct our experience. Properly understood, our ordinary life is seen to be a "waking dream" subject to many of the same conditions of our "sleeping dreams." Learning to wake up within our dreams, and see and understand deeply and clearly what is going on, can be a profound path of awakening. As Thoreau said, "Our truest life is when we are in our dreams awake."

Ask yourself, "How do I know what reality is? In my dream last night, I believed it was reality, I felt it, I experienced it, I was moved by it. Then I woke up and discarded these beliefs. How do I distinguish the real from the unreal? Where is last night's dream now? Where is yesterday's experience?" In a similar way, you can reflect upon the waking state as a dream. If you see that nighttime dreams and daytime illusions are the same, this can reduce compulsiveness and suffering.

As you begin to understand the relativity of your waking life and to experience it more as a dream that is "relatively" true, you will become more receptive to new possibilities and interpretations. Dreams are partial realities, ultimately unreal, illusory. You can see that your situation may not be quite as serious as you thought. This may shift your sense of self, improve your relationships, and help you to live with greater freedom, compassion, and creativity. There are different ways to go from the unquestioned delusions of ordinary life to a state of spiritual maturity, but learning to regard existence as being dreamlike is one of the most enjoyable and interesting paths.

For most of our lives we have viewed the world as real, solid, and concrete. Learning to see it in a whole different light can be very enlightening. Everything becomes easier. This helps us to lighten up, to be kinder, to hold both the good and the bad more lightly as fleeting, insubstantial, dreamlike experiences. We begin to sense what infinity may be—infinite time, infinite space, infinite consciousness, infinite possibilities. As you learn to look, listen, and reflect more deeply, you penetrate and deconstruct the layers of illusion and begin to behold reality in its true mystery and magnificence. Approaching life in this way, everyday experience becomes a source of endless joy and delight.

Dream yoga practice begins with the understanding that the more present and awake you are in your life, the more present and awake you can become in your sleeping dreams. If in your waking life you allow your mind to be undisciplined, impulsive, driven by mindless habit, what do you expect to find in your dreams? As you develop greater mindfulness and self-discipline, and learn to focus and understand your mind, it will be more likely that in your dreams you will be better able to harness the power of your mind to gain deeper insight into the nature of reality.

There are four foundations of dream yoga meditation that are practiced while you are awake. The first is to regard your waking perceptions—what you see, hear, smell, taste, and touch—as a dream. It's as if you say to yourself, "Isn't this an interesting dream experience!" and really believe it to be so. This sets up an inclination in the mind that can be activated in your dreams to regard ordinary and dream experiences as ephemeral, illusory, insubstantial projections and constructions of the mind. Recognizing this within a dream will awaken a strong experience of lucidity and presence. So the first foundation is to regard waking life as a dream.

The second foundation is to begin to reduce the reactivity of your mind—your tendency toward attraction and repulsion while you are awake. When you notice your mind is drawn toward a pleasant sound, smell, taste, touch, or sight, remind yourself that the object, your reaction to the object, and your very sense of self are all a dream, a construction of the mind. Beginning to demagnetize your compulsiveness and reactivity in waking life will free you to be more awake, open, and creative in your dreams.

The third foundation for dream yoga practice takes place just before you go to sleep. It has two phases. First, review the day by allowing memories and images of the day to arise in your mind. As they do, regard all of these memories as being like a dream. Then, on the basis of this recognition, shift to phase two and generate a strong determination to vividly and clearly recognize your sleeping dreams as also being dreams. As you go to sleep, hold this strong intention to be mindful of your dreaming, and pray for help and inspiration to remember your intention.

The fourth foundation is to rejoice and be grateful upon waking up if you were actually able to have a clear and lucid dream. Let your successes deepen your confidence and rejoice. Let your failures to be mindful of your dreams help you to strengthen your determination to recognize your dreams, and strengthen your prayers that you might awaken within your dreams.

It can also be helpful before you go to sleep to do some meditation to clear the mind and purify some of the negativity or emotional turbulence that has accumulated during the day. Practice deep relaxation and the loving-kindness meditation, or the radiant being meditation, or any other practices that are helpful to calm and clear the mind.

The actual practice of dream yoga is to recognize and transform the ordinary habits of the mind and to release the mind from its limitations into a wholesome and boundless display of our innate creativity and compassion. One technique is to practice multiplying things in a dream. If in a dream you see a flower or a tree, mentally multiply it so that there are a dozen, or a thousand, or a limitless number of flowers or trees filling the vastness of space.

The classic texts outline eleven categories of ordinary mental experience that are transformed through the practice of dream yoga. These involve the multiplication of objects; the "morphing" of the size of an object—making it bigger or smaller; changing the quantity or quality of the objects in the dream; modulating the experience of movement by speeding things up and slowing things down within the dream; transforming things into other things; emanating rays of light and other things from one's body; traveling from place to place; and generating a boundless array of extraordinary experiences. All of these are ways of stretching the mind to realize its infinite creative potential which is normally eclipsed by habit. As the mind becomes more open, flexible, and supple, we discover a new freedom of mind and come to better understand how we construct the illusion of our ordinary experiences.

A word of caution: Remember that developing the foundations for dream yoga in your waking life can protect you from getting too fascinated and attached to the experiences you create in your dreams. This is especially important as some people who practice less grounded traditions of lucid dreaming run the risk of being seduced by their own creations, and actually reinforcing some of the negative habits of the mind. As with all meditation practices, beginning dream yoga practice with the Taking Refuge meditation (page 41) will help ensure that the meditation will be most beneficial and effective.

Dream yoga is a very profound practice that is also regarded as a training in staying conscious at the time of death and in making the transition from this life onto the path of awakening to your True Nature. It is said that to awaken to your True Nature at death, you must first learn to awaken fully within deep, dreamless sleep. To awaken within dreamless sleep, you must learn to awaken within your dreams. And to awaken with your dreams, you must learn to be mindfully present and awake to the illusory display of your daily life. Taken to heart, this advice helps us recognize that the practice of mindfulness itself opens the way for us to be present in every experience of our life, and perhaps beyond.

THE CENTER OF YOUR MANDALA

In every system of sacred art and science we find reference to methods of generating a sphere of sacred space. This space is often represented as a mandala, a medicine wheel, Neolithic stone circles, round stained glass windows in cathedrals, or other sacred symbols. Each has a center and a periphery. Each serves as a tool for contemplation guiding the mind to recognize and participate more fully in the dynamic interplay of forces within and around us.

Sitting comfortably and at ease, breathe and draw the universe into you. Breathing out from the nucleus of your inner mandala, feel yourself sitting at the center of your universe. Remember that you are always at the center of your world, wherever you go. And remember that every single being likewise abides at the center of their own mandala. Interpenetrating spheres of energy and consciousness fill space with an intricate latticework of mandalas generated from the nucleus of each atom and each being. Each being is embracing and is embraced by all others.

Sit firm, confident, and serene at the center of your mandala of energy and awareness. And if any experience knocks you off center, simply breathe and draw yourself back to the center.

THE DROP AND THE OCEAN

And I have felt a presence that disturbs me with the
joy of elevated thoughts; a sense sublime of something
far more deeply interfused, whose dwelling is the light
of setting suns, and the round ocean and the living air,
and the blue sky, and in the mind of man; a motion
and a spirit, that impels all thinking things, all
objects of all thought, and rolls through all things.

—William Wordsworth

Quietly and comfortably now, allow the breath to freely come and flow, effortlessly releasing and dissolving thoughts and tensions into space.

As you inhale, imagine a bubble of light-energy filling you from within. As you exhale, imagine this bubble expanding . . . opening and expanding out into the space around you. With each breath, be filled by this luminous energy, and with each exhalation, imagine this sphere of light-energy opening and expanding, moving freely through the space, the walls, the buildings, the earth around you. Let everything open. Let your small sense of self expand and open to your surroundings. Allow all of the feelings and sensations and vibrations within your body to expand, open, and dissolve like a cloud melting into space. Use the breath to help you learn to expand your sphere of energy awareness like the expanding circle of a pebble dropped into a still pool . . . *ahhh* . . . opening . . . opening . . . in all directions . . . filling the space above you, filling the space below you, expanding and opening out before you, behind you opening and expanding as a sphere of energy-life-awareness all around you . . . opening and expanding with each breath.

Now as you inhale, allow this light-energy to take on a pleasing color and sense-quality—perhaps blue and peaceful, or red and warm, or any color-feeling combination that feels right to you. Allow this feeling and color to fill you deeply and then, as you exhale, allow the color-feeling sphere to open and expand within and around you. Imagine filling the space around you with luminous waves of warmth and well-being. Imagine generating an atmosphere of peace, happiness, and good vibrations that pervades the world around you. Sitting quietly, simply allow this wellspring of inner energy to come alive, open, and expand around you so that anyone near you can receive the benefit.

Now, having established this expansive sense of well-being, imagine that as your sphere of energy awareness opens and expands, there is an echo from the universe at large. Imagine that as your drop or nucleus of energy expands outward, a vast ocean of peace, warmth, and love converges and pours into you. Simultaneously now, experience this feeling of expansion and convergence. Your tiny mind-drop opening outward, and dissolving into a vast spacious ocean, and this ocean of positive energy vibration flowing, and converging into your drop. Allow all of your limitations, pains, thoughts, and cares to be dissolved into this free-flowing convergence.

This variation is an excellent technique for dissolving emotional pain as well:

As you exhale, allow the energy or feeling of the pain to open out and dissolve into space. As the energy vibration of the pain expands, sense or vividly imagine feeling a healing echo of energy-vibration pouring into you from the energy-ocean surrounding you. Feel this healing wave flowing into you and dissolving into the region of the pain. For example, when you experience a sense of burning, allow that feeling to expand while simultaneously a cool, soothing energy is drawn back into you. If you are feeling agitated, allow that feeling to open, expand, and dissipate while at the same time you feel deep peace pouring into you, flooding you completely with well-being. Allow yourself to receive from the universe-at-large whatever you most need at this time.

Breathing out, give yourself permission to let go of the knots of tension that block your body, fog your mind, and close your heart. Let everything within you open into harmony. Allow the breath to naturally and effortlessly bathe your tissues in oxygen and light that dissolves the tension or pain. Allow the waves of breath to fill you with the love, courage, and strength you need to let go of tension, to let go of fear, to release doubt or anger, and to rest in your own wholeness.

Breathing and receiving what you need . . . releasing the old limitations . . . resting in wholeness . . . tune into whatever frequency of positive healing qualities that you need at this time. . . .

SPHERE OF LIGHT

If for a moment we make way with our petty selves,
wish no ill to anyone, apprehend no ill, cease to be
but as a crystal which reflects a ray—what shall
we not reflect! What a universe will appear
crystallized and radiant around us.

—*Henry David Thoreau*

Sitting quietly with your eyes closed or slightly open, imagine a luminous sphere of light, like the sun, shining in the space in front and above you. Let this sphere be an idealized representation of all the mental, physical, emotional, and spiritual qualities you most wish to energize and embody in your life at this time. Vividly imagine that you are soaking up all the rays of this light source and its energy of relaxation, calm, clarity, and inner strength, as though you were sunbathing. Feel these rays soaking into you, pervading your body and mind—more deeply and completely with each breath. Let these feelings of calmness, inner strength, and harmony grow and glow deeply within you.

Now imagine that this shining luminous sphere sends light tendrils out to all corners of the universe, to all the sources of inspiration, healing, and harmonizing energy you need at this time. Imagine these rays of light drawing back into this sphere all the healing and harmonizing power that exists throughout space and time. It all pours back into your shining sphere of light, charging it up into a crystal that showers you with the light of a billion shining suns. Now imagine this brilliant light-energy streaming into you, completely dissolving all your tension and pain, all your worries and cares, healing and opening the places in your body, heart, and mind that need to become whole. Feel the inner clouds of darkness vanish in this flood of brilliant light. Feel the fog of sluggishness and dullness dissolve completely into a vitalized calm within.

Imagine this shining sphere of light coming closer now, pouring its light down into you. Let it come to the top of your head. Feel a shower of cleansing, healing, purifying light flooding you, washing you completely clean and clear throughout. Vividly imagine your body as a crystal flooded with rainbow light. Now imagine this light pouring through you, shining from your heart through your eyes, through the pores of your skin. Flowing out into the world. Tidal waves of healing, helpful, crystal, rainbow-like light shining to you. Flowing through you and into the world.

Now, if you like, imagine this luminous sphere coming down into you like a glorious, brilliant supernova of powerful rainbow light slipping into a crystal sea, merging and melting into the luminous open space within you. Imagine that it transforms your body and mind into a vast, open state of unimpeded clarity and luminosity, and that your emotions are transformed into power, harmony, generosity, and confidence.

Experience yourself as a radiant being. Feel this deep vital energy flowing deeply through you and out into the world. Experience the peaceful power of this way of seeing yourself. Imagine that these waves of positive feeling are like clear rainbow light that can reach out to others in ways that bring relief, inspiration, energy, or whatever else they may need. Wherever you direct your attention, let there be blessings.

RADIANT BEING

Hovering in the space above and before you, envision and affirm the presence of a luminous, loving being of light. This may be envisioned as a radiant Buddha, as a great teacher, or a saint.

Now from the heart of this being of light before you, imagine rays of light reaching out through the vastness of space and time to reach the hearts of all the great and awakened beings throughout the entire universe. Imagine that these rays of light draw the energy, wisdom, power, love, blessings, and presence of all those great beings back into the being visualized before you, and that as this happens your own visualization becomes empowered and enlivened by the blessings of all these beings.

The luminous, loving being gazes upon you with a peaceful, tender mercy and compassion, with the utmost love.

Rest in the radiant field of blessings as though you are sunbathing. As the light fills you, imagine it purifying all the darkness of ignorance within you and bringing you to a state of clarity and luminosity.

Now imagine that from the crown of this luminous loving being rays of white light shine and pour into the crown of your head and flow through your entire body. This blissful white light purifies and transforms all the harmful habits and tendencies that are knotted in your body. It restores your wholeness, replenishes your vitality, purifies your diseases, heals your wounds, and neutralizes any latencies for disease that may be within you. It renews and revitalizes your nervous system and clarifies your senses.

In a similar way, envision that from the throat center of this luminous being blissful rays of red light radiate and enter into your own throat center. This red light purifies all the negativity of your speech and communications, transforms all your bad habits of lying, exaggerating, slandering others, speaking harshly of others, and all your mindless idle talk that only wastes your breath and vitality. This radiant red blessing light purifies your speech and awakens your capacity for your voice to become an instrument for expressing truth, compassion, and goodness.

Next, from the heart of this blessed being infinite waves of blue light radiate, pouring into your own heart center, purifying and transforming your mind and transforming all your ignorance and confusion into wisdom and compassion. Your limited sense of self dissolves and you awaken to your own deep True Nature and potential. The mental poisons of ignorance, greed, hatred, jealousy, and pride are transformed into a rainbow of enlightened wisdom and love. Purified in this way, your heart becomes like a clear radiant jewel with a pure white lotus blossom at its center.

The being of light before you grows smaller and brighter and then comes to sit and shine brightly in this lotus within your heart-center. Throughout the day, whenever you eat or drink anything, let it become an offering to this luminous presence at the core of your innermost being. As you walk and talk, carry the divine dignity of this sacred presence within you and move through the world like a lighthouse of love radiating blessings to all beings.

Imagine that the light shining from your innermost luminous heart touches and awakens the luminous loving presence in the hearts of all beings, and that through the power of these blessings the beings of light within them begin to shine more brightly as a radiant blessing for the world and an inspiration for all beings.

RESTORING THE WORLD TO WHOLENESS

As the wish for well-being, not just for ourselves but for all beings, awakens in our hearts, we participate in a profound teaching from the Kabbalah on restoring wholeness to the world. This is called *tikkun ha-olam* in Hebrew, which means, "repairing the world." Tikkun means to mend or repair. Outwardly, tikkun is associated with social action that has the goal of improving the world. But inwardly, in the esoteric traditions, tikkun is the sacred inner work of mending a broken world and restoring it to wholeness through spiritually developing the love that carries us beyond our separate self. Tikkun is regarded as the highest, most profound purpose of our life.

This activity to restore balance and harmony in our world is closely akin to the Buddhist notion of *bodhichitta*, "the spirit of awakening," which holds that at the heart-core of every living being is a universal impulse to fully awaken to the wholeness of its potential and to serve others in their awakening.

The work of awakening and repairing is an inside-out job. It is said that every tiny bit of restoration of wholeness within ourselves directly contributes to the restoration and awakening of all beings and of the whole world. The impulse of every movement toward healing, every moment of mindfulness, every act of kindness we generate within ourselves, is directly shared or transmitted to support the emergence of that potential within each and every living being.

The more fully awake we are, the better equipped we are and the more natural it is for us to reach out and nurture the emergence of greater harmony in our world. As our awareness and sensitivity increase, we recognize that certain situations in our life or world are intolerably unproductive, toxic, or destructive. This helps to strengthen our resolve to get healthier; resolve conflicts; put a stop to abusive violence in our relationships; and become an advocate, activist, or celebrant of noble causes that expand the sphere of balance and harmony to our world and to the lives of others.

The following meditation can help you bring this idea more alive. Imagine that you are standing on a mountaintop on a still, clear, dark night. In the sky around you are an infinite number of jewels linked together in a subtle network of light. Imagine now, as you light a little candle, that instantly its light and warmth is reflected in each and every one of the jewels surrounding you. Not only that, but each of the jewels is also illumined by the light that is reflected in it from all the illuminating jewels. It is a fantastic and inspiring sight. Now imagine that as you light up a moment of mindfulness within you, the light of that mindfulness "lights up" all living beings. Likewise, if within yourself you awaken or light up a moment of love, gratitude, wonder, joy, forgiveness, that impulse immediately lights up within all others. The transmission is effortless, immediate, heart to heart.

Each of the jewels in the net is lighting up all the other jewels, giving rise to waves of excitement, waves of sympathy, waves of gratitude, love, or blessings.

In each moment we are awake, we can feel what is reverberating within ourselves and respond in a way that lights up the world in either a weird or a wonderful way. In moments of distraction, when mindlessness sets in, the momentum of habit propels us. In moments of mindfulness, we at least have a choice.

As we learn to recognize and repair the rifts in our own life we reestablish wholeness within ourselves. As our internal repair work deepens, we are better able to reach out—inwardly and outwardly—to repair the world around us. As we focus the flow of our dynamic being more into balance, and dissolve the rigid boundaries that separate us from our wholeness, we restore the world to balance. These aren't just nice ideas but a description of the way things are. Our journey of awakening is one of learning to bring more of our natural, clear, lucid, loving, radiant presence into our world. This is very deep tikkun.

TRANSFORMATIVE VISION

The tower is as wide and spacious as the sky itself....
And within this tower, spacious and exquisitely
ornamented, there are hundreds of thousands ...
of towers, each one of which is as exquisitely
ornamented as the main tower itself and as
spacious as the sky. And all of the towers, beyond
calculation in number, stand not at all in one
another's way, each preserves its individual
existence in perfect harmony with all the rest; ...
there is a state of perfect intermingling and yet of

perfect orderliness . . . the young pilgrim sees himself
in all the towers as well as in each single tower
where all is contained in one and each contains all.

—*Avatamsaka Sutra*

The following sequence of images and short meditations invite you to bring a more creative mind to transforming the many ordinary activities of daily life.

We once spent some time with a Native American teacher named Thundercloud who taught us a beautiful water medicine prayer-blessing. When you drink water, you pray, "May this water as it flows through me become medicine, and strengthen the earth, and purify, and bring food for people, and renew the people." Can you imagine how it would change your life if at least sometimes during the day when you turned on the faucet, drank water, or urinated, you were to remember this prayer?

The classic practices of the *lojung* or "thought transformation" teachings in the Mahayana Buddhist tradition also offer many creative meditations to transform every ordinary act into a gesture of creative universal compassion. For example: You can drink a cup of water to quench your thirst; or you can mindfully drink a cup of water and transform it with a prayer and a creative meditation into a bowl of healing nectar; or you can drink a cup of water with the prayer and motivation that by drinking this water, and quenching your thirst, may the thirst of all beings be quenched and fulfilled by this simple act.

You can walk out a door mindlessly. You can walk out a door mindfully. You can walk out a door with the wish, prayer, affirmation, and visualization that as you walk out that door you lead all beings from darkness into light, from limitation into the boundless space of infinite freedom and potential. When you close the door, meditate that the possibility of returning to ignorance and delusion is sealed forever, for all beings. Similarly, as you come in from outside, you can do it mindlessly, mindfully, or as a gesture and affirmation of leading people from being lost in the confusion of their outer lives into the deep, clear, lucid, loving presence of their innermost being.

You can sweep the walk or wash the windows with disdain for all the dirt and debris, or you can sweep and clean as though you were actually purifying and polishing your mind and bringing forth the unobstructed clarity and purity of your innermost being.

Though such meditations may or may not actually have an outward effect on the world, they are powerful for opening and transforming your own mind and brain, making them more fit instruments to hold the dazzling reality of the potential within creation. They can also open your heart, burst the bubble of your own implosive self-centeredness and help you to live in a more loving, caring, and compassionate way. They can help you awaken a sincere wish in your heart that your life will in some small way reduce suffering and be helpful and comforting for others.

Once, when we were walking with Thich Nhat Hanh, he said, "Every mindful step you take, I take with you." Imagine that as you walk you hold the hand of a beloved teacher, or teachers. As you do, envision them holding the hands of their teachers who hold the hands of their teachers who hold the hands of their teachers. Draw strength and inspiration by affirming this deep connection.

When you say a prayer, chant a mantra, or do a ritual, can you imagine and affirm that you join in spirit with all those who have ever recited that prayer or chanted that mantra or performed that ritual throughout time? As you do these things, you receive the blessings and the inspirations from them all into yourself while at the same time radiating and redistributing and affirming those blessings through you to all beings. As you light the Shabbat candles on Friday night, can you feel the spirit and the blessings of all your mothers and grandmothers? As you receive Holy Communion, can you bring alive and affirm your spiritual solidarity with countless people throughout time in the one body of Christ? As you watch the sunrise and welcome a new day, can you imagine looking out through the eyes of countless people, throughout the ages, marveling with gratitude at the Great Mystery that continually renews and sustains your life?

The great *Avatamsaka Sutra,* the "Flower Ornament Sutra," is perhaps the world's most elaborate text for "seeding" creative meditations. It offers many mind-expanding images of the nature of the fully enlightened mind, including the following description of the ten wisdoms of a *bodhisattva,* a being who is committed to fully awakening to their True Nature and potential in order to help all beings to awaken as well. At a certain stage in such a being's spiritual evolution, they are able to:

> Bring all beings' bodies into one body, and one body into all beings' bodies; to bring all inconceivable aeons into one moment, and one moment into all aeons; to bring all sacred things into one thing and one sacred thing into all things; to bring an inconceivable number of places into one place, and to bring one place into an inconceivable number of places...to make all thoughts into one thought, and one thought into all thoughts; to bring all voices and languages into one voice and language, and one voice and language into all voices and languages; to bring the past-present-future into one time, and one time into the past-present-future.

Remember, your motivation, creative vision of possibilities, and prayer will determine the actual effect of your meditation. Every action of your life provides an opportunity for awakening.

MANTRA: RADIANT BLESSINGS
AND PROTECTION FOR THE MIND

Over the years, we've been introduced to the use of mantra or devotional chanting in every meditative tradition we've studied. The actual word mantra means "mind protection." While engaged in chanting a mantra, your mind is protected from dissipating its clarity and power in random or negative thoughts. In many meditative traditions, formal periods of quiet contemplative practice are preceded by a time of devotional chanting or mantric repetition. The repetitive and often sacred nature of these chants have a calming and stabilizing effect which builds coherence and power in the mind and the central nervous system.

The use of such "mind protectors" is an ancient and powerful sacred science. The inner scientist knows and understands the use of sound and vibration as a tool to evoke and refine specific qualities of mind. In Native American traditions, a young man or woman would be sent on a vision quest and told to listen for a sacred song which the Great Spirit would teach them during this time of alert, receptive vigilance. After days of fasting, prayer, or other ordeals, a chant would emerge into awareness as a gift or sign from the Great Spirit. From that time on, this special chant would be used to steady and protect the mind at critical times. Having practiced this chant in the face of adversity millions of times over the course of your life, you would turn to it wholeheartedly and single-pointedly when approaching the moment of death, allowing it to carry you across the threshold between worlds and into the vastness of Spirit.

The actual practice of mantra meditation can be quite simple. You can just sit quietly and mentally recite a mantra or meaningful phrase, resting the mind on its sound or inner resonance within you. Whenever your mind wanders, simply return to the repetition and keep your attention on what you are doing. To elaborate on this method, visualize waves of light and good vibrations pouring from your heart to others, bringing more light, love, and happiness into the world and dissolving the darkness, pain, and fear that fills the minds of so many beings. Imagine that as the sound, vibration, and heartfelt intent of your chanting reaches out, it draws back into you waves of inspiring strength and blessings.

Rabbi Theodore Falcon introduced us to a Hebrew prayer that is used as a mantra: *Shiviti Adonai L'negdi Tamid.* One way of translating this ancient formula is, "When I bring myself into balance, God is before me always." Taken to heart, this formula can be the seed of a profound contemplation that can inspire you to behold the sacred in every activity of your life. Reciting this prayer, in English or in Hebrew, let your mind grow more calm, clear, and balanced. Held in this spirit, reciting the Rosary, the Lord's Prayer, or the *Sh'ma* prayer, or chanting a Sufi Zikr or the mantra *Om Mani Padme Hum,* or even chanting "Peace, Love, Kindness" will likely offer similar results. Sitting quietly, resting in the flow of your breathing, allow your recitation to carry you more and more deeply into radiant peace. Looking out from deep within, let your eyes truly be windows for your soul and behold the world as sacred and alive with spirit. Sitting, walking, driving, talking, alone or with others, allow your sense of inner balance to deepen and behold the Mystery, sacred majesty, and Presence of the world's radiance shining deep within and around you.

When you have a feeling for it, the chanting of a mantra can help to calm and focus the mind when you are busy in the world. It is a simple and effective method for strengthening and developing positive qualities of the mind in moments that are ordinarily wasted—driving to work, waiting in line, being "on hold" on the telephone, walking down the street, and so on—all ordinary activities can be easily integrated into your meditation practice.

This practice of the inner essence of mind protection is more a state of mind that a vocalization. In its deepest essence, it is a state of heart and mind that recognizes the nonduality and interdependent relationship of all beings and things. The response to this is the wisdom that spontaneously wishes to contribute to the well-being of others. This can be demonstrated not only through kind words and helpful actions, but through a resonance of heart and mind that reaches out to others in a deep, quiet, and loving way.

When the mind is busy or directed toward superficial appearances, simply chanting a mantra with the intention of creating a more positive atmosphere in the world within and around you can be very helpful. As your mind becomes more subtle and quiet, the repetition of the mantra may likewise become more subtle, until you rest in its innermost essence—silent prayer, a way of simply being natural that brings peace to the world within and around you. In this way, mantra and spoken prayer merge into silence and become the prayer of the heart.

PRAYERS OF THE HEART

Contemplative prayer, rightly understood, is the normal development of grace . . . it is the opening of mind and heart—our whole being—to God beyond thoughts, words, and emotions. Moved by God's preeminent grace, we open our awareness to God whom we know by faith is within us, closer than breathing, closer than thinking, closer than choosing—closer than consciousness itself. Contemplative prayer is a process of interior transformation, a relationship initiated by God and leading, if we consent, to divine union.

—Father Thomas Keating

We live in a responsive universe. If you drop a stone in a pond, it both sends out and draws in ripples. Through heartfelt and sincere prayer, the energy of our receptivity and intent extends, creating a reverberation in our deep psyche that reaches out to the Mystery and draws back the inspiration and blessing energy that may help us. Especially in times of great chaos and perturbation, centering prayer can offer a sense of stability, meaning, direction, inspiration, balance, harmony, healing, and faith.

Remembering that even minute changes in the "equations" driving how order manifests out of chaos, we can imagine how making even subtle shifts in the quality of our intentions, beliefs, prayers, attitudes, and values can potentially create dramatic, even miraculous, changes in the quality of our lives.

When you see beauty in your world, let your heart reach out with gratitude and rejoicing to bless that beauty. When you encounter or hear about suffering, cruelty, and pain, allow it crack your heart open to a prayer of healing and compassion for that suffering. Taking the world to heart at every moment becomes an invitation for the radiance of our prayers of gratitude, blessings, and compassion. These are not only prayers put in words, but in the prayers of our heart that are silent, wordless, deep, and immediate in their activation of our deep presence that dwells within the deepest heart of our humanity.

As our kind teacher Lama Thubten Yeshe would remind us, "Silent meditation, without thoughts, totally open, awake, and aware, this is absolute prayer!" A profound understanding of prayer is offered by Father Thomas Keating:

> The goal of contemplative prayer is not so much the emptiness of thoughts or conversations as the emptiness of self. In contemplative prayer, one ceases to multiply reflections and acts of will. A different kind of knowledge rooted in love emerges in which the awareness of God's presence supplants the awareness of one's own presence and the inveterate tendency to reflect on self. The experience of God's presence gradually frees one from making oneself or one's relationship with God the center of the universe.

MATRIX OF MIND

The following meditation can open the way to a direct and profound insight into the nature of mind and perceived phenomena.

Envision a luminous sphere spontaneously and effortlessly appearing in the space before you. Allow its luminous clarity to pervade the surrounding space with a sense of both luminous clarity and "knowingness."

Next, envision similar spheres of luminous knowingness spontaneously and naturally emerging from the space above and below to either side of the original sphere, thus forming a cluster of five. Now envision that each of these secondary spheres becomes the center of another cluster, and that each of those becomes the nucleus of another cluster, until the whole space is pervaded by a unified field of luminous knowingness.

Another approach to this meditation is to envision a sphere of luminous knowingness spontaneously arising at your own center of mindbody. Sense and feel its luminous knowingness pervading the whole space within and around you. Envision in the field of space surrounding you that similar spheres of luminous clarity emerge before you, behind you, to your left and right, as well as above and behind you. Each of these spheres is identical and all together they form a matrix of seven, with six clustered around the central sphere. Beginning with the sphere before you, envision this sphere now becoming the center of a similar cluster with six around it. Then one by one, allow each of the primary spheres around you to become the center of a new cluster, a higher order of luminous, knowing spheres. Continue to multiply these lights out in clusters of six spheres, each of which become the nucleus for a further cluster, until the whole space within and surrounding you is pervaded by a unified matrix of knowing luminosity.

Bring an effortless and quietly joyful mind to this meditation. Avoid struggling or trying too hard to get it right, but simply practice again and again until it becomes effortless to multiply these luminous spheres and establish this matrix of mind.

Practice dissolving yourself and the world into this unified clarity. As sights, sounds, colors, and other phenomena begin to emerge within and around you, allow each new experience, whether sensory or mental, to be regarded as a spontaneous, selfless, creative play of mind.

Through this meditation you may come to know mind as intimately pervading and unifying the field of your experience. Within this matrix of mind, know that you can loosen your need for an "I" or "experiencer" that stands separate from others and from perceived objects. Though appearances may continue to appear distinct and separate from you, gradually the practice of this meditation will reveal that the nature of mind and the world it perceives is actually nondual and intimately related.

> *Awareness is like a beam of light that shines*
> *endlessly into space. We only perceive that light when*
> *it is reflected off some object and consciousness is pro-*
> *duced . . . Awareness is the light by which we see the*
> *world . . . We mistake the clear light of pure awareness*
> *for the shadows that it casts in consciousness . . . We*
> *forget that we are the light itself and imagine that*
> *we are the densities that reflect the light back to us.*

—Stephen Levine

SEVEN
HEART-CENTERED MEDITATION

Some day, after we have mastered the winds,
the waves, the tides, and gravity, we shall
harness the energies of love. Then, for
the second time in the history of the world,
humankind will have discovered fire.

—Teilhard de Chardin

TTHE FOLLOWING HEART-CENTERED MEDITATIONS are woven of many themes. In them you will recognize elements of concentration, mindfulness, reflective, and creative meditations. We have gathered these all together here to help bring your awareness to the many methods for awakening the love and compassion that are born of the wisdom of deep relationship.

MEDITATION ON GRATITUDE

Both ancient teachings and modern medical research agree that one of the quickest, most direct routes to restoring harmony and balance in our lives is to foster gratitude and appreciation. The moment you shift from a mindstate of negativity or judgment to one of appreciation, there are immediate effects at many levels of your being: brain function becomes more balanced, harmonized, and supple; your heart begins to pump in a much more coherent and harmonious rhythm; and biochemical changes trigger a host of healthful balancing reactions throughout your body.

In the healing ways of indigenous people, the restorative power of gratitude was well understood. A heart filled with gratitude generates actions and prayers that complete the circle between the gift offered to us, the receiver of the gift, and the sacred source of the gift. To offer prayers of thanksgiving is a gesture of rejoicing in discovering the many gifts that life brings us. Here is a practice we often teach as a way to dwell in gratitude and thanksgiving:

Sitting quietly, shift toward dynamic balance with a few minutes of mindful breathing. Bring to mind someone for whom you are deeply grateful. As you breathe in, take this person to heart. Breathing out, let your heartfelt gratitude shine deeply and brightly to them and through them. Continue for as long as you like, letting each breath take to heart a loved one, a friend, someone who has been kind to you, someone who is teaching you patience or how to forgive. Let each breath shine from the depths of your being through the depths of their being in order to light up their life with your love. Taking your eyes, your ears, your hands, your intelligence to heart, bless them in a similar way with the heartfelt radiance of your appreciation. Whoever or whatever comes to mind, gather them into your heart, one at a time or all together. Taking these many gifts to heart, complete and affirm the circle with gratitude, assuring that the stream of blessings in your life and in the universe will be unbroken.

MEDITATION ON FORGIVENESS

As we develop our practice of meditation we naturally become more conscious of what is going on in our own minds. We become clearer about what we feel and why. We start to uncover the discrepancies in our lives, and get in touch with the bruises and hurts of old relationships. Slowly, we are able to tie loose ends and heal old wounds.

Forgiveness meditation is a wonderful way to heal the pain of old hurts that block our hearts and prevent us from trusting and loving ourselves and others. Forgiveness is the key to opening our hearts, to learning from the painful lessons of the past in order to move into the future unhindered.

Begin by sitting quietly, relaxing your body and focusing your mind with the breath. Allow memories and images and emotions to float freely in your mind, no matter how painful they are—things you have done, said, and thought for which you have not forgiven yourself.

From your heart say to yourself, "I forgive myself for whatever I may have done in the past, intentionally or unintentionally, by my actions, my words, and my thoughts that caused me pain. I have suffered enough! I have learned and grown and I am ready now to open my heart to myself. May I be happy, may I be free from confusion, may I know the work of truly understanding myself, others, and the world. May I come to know my own wholeness and fullness and help others to do the same."

Now, in the space in front of you, imagine a person you love whom you want to forgive or whose forgiveness you need. From your heart to theirs, directly communicate this intention: "With all my heart I forgive you for whatever you may have done, intentionally or unintentionally, by your actions, your words, or thoughts, that have caused me pain.

I forgive you, and I ask that you forgive me for whatever I may have done, intentionally or unintentionally, by my actions, words, or thoughts, that caused you pain. Please forgive me. May you be happy, free, and joyful. May we both open our hearts and minds to meet in love and understanding as we grow into our wholeness." Imagine that this message is received and accepted, and affirm the feeling of healing between you. Then let this person's image melt into space.

Now, in the space in front of you imagine someone toward whom you feel great resentment or negativity. To the best of your ability and from your heart to theirs, communicate the essence of the following: "From my heart I forgive you for whatever you have done, intentionally or unintentionally, that has caused me pain. I forgive you for the actions, words, and thoughts you have expressed from your own pain, confusion, insensitivity, and fear. I forgive you, and I ask that you forgive me for the way in which I have, intentionally or unintentionally, closed my heart to you. I ask your forgiveness for causing you suffering. May you be happy. May you be free from suffering and confusion. May we both open our hearts to meet in love and understanding as we grow into our wholeness." Imagine that this message has been received and accepted, and affirm the healing that has taken place within you and between the two of you. Then allow the image to melt into space.

Now think about the countless people toward whom you have closed your heart. Remember how you felt and what you did when people abused you, spoke harshly, took "your" parking space, crowded in front of you in line, *ad infinitum.* . . . Consider how many people you have hurt in some way by your own conscious or unconscious actions, words, and thoughts. How many times have you been the abuser, the one who crowded in, the one who spoke harshly? Imagine these countless beings standing before you. From your heart to theirs generate the essence of the following: "I forgive you for whatever you have done, intentionally or unintentionally, that has caused me to suffer. I forgive you and ask you to forgive me for whatever I have done, intentionally or unintentionally, that has hurt you. May you and I and all of us create the causes for happiness in our lives. May we outgrow and transform the causes of our suffering. May we all come to know the joy of truly understanding and experiencing our interrelationship. May we open our hearts and minds to each other and meet in harmony."

Repeat this reflective meditation as often as you like. At the conclusion, imagine and feel as vividly and wholeheartedly as you are able that you have actually released all guilt and blame toward yourself. In this present moment, allow yourself to feel forgiveness and a patient acceptance of your past actions.

LOVING-KINDNESS MEDITATION

Love is that flame that once kindled burns
everything, and only the mystery
and the journey remain.

—Rumi

Another very simple yet potent practice you can do on a daily basis to revitalize your interconnectedness at a deep level is the practice of radiant love. We especially like to do this one at the end or start of a day, or to celebrate and share the joy of a job well done or a moment well lived, and let it ripple out to the larger community we're part of in a boundless way. The essence of this reflective prayer and meditation for the cultivation of loving-kindness is the wish that we, and all beings, enjoy happiness and well-being. In Sanskrit, loving-kindness is called *maitri*, which is often translated as "unconditional friendliness." Here's how it goes:

Begin by touching your heart, if you like, and smile to yourself in tender appreciation and care. Holding the sincere wish to be of benefit to yourself and others, take a few deep breaths, relax your body, and bring your awareness to the area in the center of your chest around your heart. Continue to breathe naturally and gently with awareness, allowing the region of your heart to open and soften with the movement of the breath flowing through it. Notice any sensations of warmth or tingling there as you deepen your calm awareness.

In this practice, also known as *metta,* we focus initially upon ourselves, recognizing that despite the unwholesome behavior to which we are still prone, and the mental distortions to which we are still subject, at our very core lies an essential purity. There is a fathomless potential within us for wisdom and compassion, and our very wish for well-being, for happiness, our wish to be free of suffering, may be regarded as an expression of that True Nature. Let it be unveiled, allowing it to manifest its full potential.

From this perspective, cultivate this prayer, aspiration, wish: "May I be free of mental distortions—free of anger, free of grasping, free of confusion. May I be free of the mental and physical suffering that arise from such distortions of the mind. And may I recognize and cultivate those other qualities of my being—loving-kindness and compassion, wisdom and patience—the whole array of wholesome qualities that are there too. For my own well-being and the well-being of others, may these arise, may these flourish. And may I experience the wonderful sense of well being and a wholesome way of life from deep compassion and from deep insight. In this way, may I be well and happy. May my fears and sorrows fall away. May I find a joy that is untainted by anxiety, a joy that comes from my own heart."

Holding the feeling of this intent and wish for well-being in your heart and mind, repeat the following phrases mentally to yourself first, several times, and then expand the radius of your loving-kindness successively out to wider and wider circles. Go deeply into the meaning and feeling behind the words:

> May I be happy and peaceful.
> May I be free from fear and pain.
> May I live with love and compassion.
> And may I fully awaken and be free.

Imagine and affirm this to be so right now, as vividly, as realistically as you can.

Now bring to mind a loved one—someone you respect and care about. When you see this person, the immediate response is one of spontaneous gladness and affection. Like yourself, this person probably has shortcomings as well, is subject to unwholesome activity and mental distortions; but this person too is endowed with True Nature and has the complete capacity for full spiritual awakening. This person, like yourself, wishes to be free of sorrow and to experience true joy. Reflecting in this way, generate the wish: "May this person, like myself, become ever freer of mental distortions and unwholesome behavior, and the sorrow, conflict, and suffering that ensue from them. And may this person find those wholesome qualities and cultivate them by whatever path most effectively nourishes him or her. For the unveiling of this person's True Nature, may this one, like myself, be truly well and happy, free of unnecessary suffering and grief."

Reaching out with your heart-mind to embrace your loved ones and friends with the energy of loving-kindness, radiate these thoughts of well-being to them in the same way:

> May you be happy and peaceful.
> May you be free from fear and pain.
> May you live with love and compassion.
> And may you fully awaken and be free.

As you hold the image of your loved ones and repeat these phrases, sense or imagine, as vividly as you can, that they are actually touched by the love radiating from your heart and that it is truly helpful for them.

Focus now on someone or a group of people toward whom you feel neutral. It might be a grocery clerk or a gas station attendant, neighbors whom you really don't know, folks you see on the way to work, or even a person you work with for whom you have no special feeling at all. Recognize that these people too, like yourself, are endowed with True Nature and, like yourself, feel suffering and joy. They may have no spiritual orientation at all, but their experiences of suffering and joy are no less real, no less important. Contemplating in this way, open the radius of your loving-kindness to encompass them as well, and extend your heartfelt prayer: "Like myself, may these persons cultivate wholesome qualities and subdue the unwholesome, and may they too be well and happy, free of unnecessary pain, grief, and fear." As you repeat these phrases again, bring these people into your heart and wish for them:

> May you be happy and peaceful.
> May you be free from fear and pain.
> May you live with love and compassion.
> And may you fully awaken and be free.

Sense or imagine that these wishes and prayers really do support them.

Now, having primed your heart-pump, turn your attention toward a person or several people toward whom your heart is closed with pain, resentment, or negativity—someone that you really don't like, whom you'd just rather not see at all, not hear at all, not even hear about. Perhaps this person has wronged you or perhaps they simply have some personality characteristics you dislike. Recognize that what we are identifying here are those very distortions, those unwholesome types of activity, that are the source of sorrow, and that this person is subject to them as are you. Just as it is not useful to identify with our own shortcomings, it is likewise not useful to identify another person with their shortcomings, distortions, or afflictions. Recognize that this person, like yourself, wishes to be happy, wishes to be free of sorrow. Maybe the ways of pursuing this goal are confused, but the wish is no less real, the experience of joy and sorrow is no less real. And if this person were to find effective means for rooting out the sources of unnecessary grief and conflict, the very reasons why you are adverse to him or her would vanish, and you would find a lovely person emerging in their place.

Consider, too, that this person or group of people, who are also searching for happiness and hoping to avoid suffering in their own lives, may at some time in the past have actually been kind to you. As you hold them in mind, be merciful with yourself. Let your own heart open to free you from the prison of imbalance you may have created for yourself out of your own anger, fear, or resentment toward the person or persons with whom you are having a hard time, or those relationships you would like to heal. With this perspective it is not hard to aspire: "May this person, like myself, be well and happy. May afflictions fall away. May this person's beauty emerge and their True Nature be unveiled." Letting your heart open to them as best you can, radiate these thoughts of loving-kindness:

> May you be happy and peaceful.
> May you be free from fear and pain.
> May you live with love and compassion.
> May you fully awaken to your greatest potential, and be free of any ignorance and confusion that leads you to act in unskillful ways.

And imagine it to be so.

Visualize yourself surrounded now by all your circles of supportive relationships, and invite into your loving awareness all the networks of support, visible and invisible, known and unknown, near and far, that make up the circle of living beings, the web of life. Expand your love and care equally to this larger field, just as the sun shines its life-giving rays equally to all. In this same way—with great equanimity to all living beings—extend the radius of your loving-kindness to all your loved ones and friends; to all the strangers or neutral people in your life; to all the people toward whom your heart has been closed; to all the humans and non-humans who search for happiness, harmony, and balance on their fleeting journeys through life. And, imagining that this vast circle of relations joins you as you open your heart to include and embrace all beings, extend the waves of loving-kindness out now in all directions:

> May all beings (or, may we all) be happy and peaceful.
> May all beings be free from fear and pain.
> May all beings live with love and compassion.
> And may all beings awaken to the light of their own
> True Nature and be free!

Let these wishes radiate to all the beings to the east. To all beings to the west; to all beings to the south; to all beings to the north. Let these wishes reach out to all beings above you and below you. To all beings in this world, in all worlds. In this time and in all times.

As you bring this meditation to a close, imagine gathering all the energy and light you have generated through this series of contemplations. Allow this quality of awareness to express itself in form by imagining a pearl of radiant, white light of the nature of purity, of the nature of loving-kindness, which is of the very essence of our own True Nature.

Imagine this pearl of radiant, brilliant, white light at your heart and, from an inexhaustible source, allow that light to suffuse every cell of your body, thoroughly saturating it with the light of loving-kindness and purification.

Now imagine the body being so filled that it is no longer able to contain this light: rays of light emerge in all directions, front and back, left and right, upward and downward. An inexhaustible source of light flows forth in all directions as an expression of your loving-kindness, your loving concern for all beings who, like yourself, aspire for happiness and wish to be free from suffering. Imagine these rays of light touching individuals all about you in your neighborhood, in your city, illuminating the environment, bringing well-being and food where there is poverty and starvation, rain where there is drought, harmony where there is conflict, peace where there is hatred. And let that light expand around the entire globe and beyond.

In this way, we dedicate and direct the merit and spiritual power of this practice not just to our own isolated, individual well-being, but to the well-being and peace of the entire world, to all beings without exception. In this way we give all that we have, and receive even more in return. If you close your meditation session at least once a day with this, it will add a greater dimension to your whole practice and will be of greater benefit to you and to the people with whom you come in contact.

After your meditation session is over, continue to carry the natural radiance of this love with you wherever you go. Let the jewel of loving-kindness and compassion shine in your heart like a luminous sun, bathing the world and all beings within it in the light of love that radiates through you as a blessing for the world. When your awareness of it fades, reenergize it by using the phrases and images offered above, and let the light of your love light up your world.

HEART TO HEART

Imagine in the space in front of you someone toward whom you feel much tenderness, friendship, love, or compassionate concern. This might evoke an image of a loved one, a close friend, even a pet. As vividly as possible, imagine the presence of this person in the space before you—either seeing them in your mind's eye or simply imagining them there before you now. Allow yourself to get in touch with the genuine sense of love and care that you feel for this being.

Now begin to focus on this person's heart—not the physical organ that pumps blood, but that center of feeling and love at the "heart" of each person. Reach out now—actually raising your arms and reaching out with your hands—and imagine cradling in your hands this person's place of deepest feeling, really touching their heart. Imagine that as you breathe in, a feeling of love and care wells up within you and fills your own heart. As you exhale, this wellspring of love within you—visualized as streams of light or energy—flows from your heart out through your arms and hands and pours gently into this person's heart. Reach out now from your heart. In a deep and silent way, offer this love and care, and imagine that it is being received by your loved one or friend in the way he or she most needs at this time.

Now, imagine that this person reaches back to touch your heart. Imagine your eyes meeting in recognition and appreciation and understanding. Imagine seeing each other with total love and forgiveness. Let any memories that block your hearts be dissolved and healed in the joy of this heart-to-heart meeting. Imagine looking deeply into one another's eyes with heartfelt love and respect and understanding. Feel the satisfaction and the intimacy of this flow between you.

Now, focus your attention on the image of your loved one or friend. Imagine the image of this person condensing into a small bright sphere of light that you tenderly hold in your hands.

As you breathe, gently place this luminous sphere in the center of your own heart. Imagine it shining brightly, like a gently glowing sun that shines with a light of love and peacefulness, dispelling any darkness within or around you.

Now, with both of your hands reach up and touch your own heart. As you breathe, imagine filling your heart with feelings of love directed toward yourself. Imagine what it is like to be here fully for yourself with the same love and care that you offer to others.

Understanding that it is difficult to receive the love and care of others if you are unable to give love even to yourself, breathe it in now. Feel the sense of genuine love for yourself well up within your entire being. Use the natural cycles of the breath to circulate this feeling of love, moving from your heart out through your arms and hands and back into your heart again. Feel what it's really like to be here for yourself.

As you establish this flow between your hands and heart, begin to extend and circulate this feeling through your whole body. With each breath send ripples of love and care from your heart out to every cell and fiber of your body, to every nook and cranny of your mind. Fill yourself with love. Fill yourself with light. Let it move and flow and circulate through every dimension of your being. Send this loving light to those regions that are in pain or that cry out for attention. Let this love flow as light to dissolve any seeds of disease that may lie hidden in your mind or body. Imagine this light vitalizing and strengthening your undeveloped potential for love, wisdom, power, and understanding.

Breathing gently now, imagine yourself filled with light, filled with love. Begin to feel the power and the presence of this love and light within you. Begin to shine it out into the world.

Resting in this vitalized state, imagine beaming your feelings of well-being and love out to dispel any darkness or fear in the world. From your heart, send ripples of this loving light, directed to your loved ones and friends, to all who live in suffering or fear, to all those leaders with the power to help or harm. Imagine this light as a beacon of love, a broadcast of caring, that will be received by others in the way that they most need to be touched at this time.

Now simply rest in the flow of the breath. Effortlessly be filled. Effortlessly extend who you are and what you have to offer, to yourself . . . to others . . . to everyone, in whatever way they need it. Radiate your own love and light out into the world. Imagine it bringing light into darkness. Imagine it fanning the powerful flames of wisdom, love, and understanding in the hearts and minds of others.

Take a moment to appreciate how the inner changes you're making within yourself are touching the world in wonderful ways. Appreciate how these quiet moments of inner work have generated an atmosphere of greater harmony, balance, and well-being in the world.

MEDITATION WITH A PARTNER

From every human being there arises a light that
reaches straight to heaven. And when two souls
destined to be together find each other, their
streams of light flow together and a single,
brighter light goes forth from the united being.

—The Baal Shem Tov

Sharing meditation time can be a powerful means of bringing depth and aliveness to our most cherished relationships. Meditating with a loved one provides an opportunity to let our conceptual and emotional dust clear in order to see each other freshly, in the ever-unfolding newness of each moment. This is the deep meaning of *respect,* which in Latin means "to look again," or to look again more deeply. In his classic teachings on meditation and prayer, Father Thomas Keating speaks to the sacredness of the deep connection between two people:

> In human relationships, as mutual love deepens, there comes a time when the two friends convey their exchanges without words. They can sit in silence sharing an experience or simply enjoying each other's presence without saying anything. Holding hands or a single word from time to time can develop this communication. This kind of relationship points to the level of interior silence that is being developed in contemplative prayer.

Though an entire volume could be devoted to the intricacies and delicacies of these "dyadic" meditations, we will briefly describe some ideas and techniques that you might enjoy exploring with a special friend. The following meditations with a partner will help you to sense and develop a more intimate and loving relationship with yourself and with those you love.

1. Attunement

   Sit across from your partner palm to palm, with your left hands facing upward and your right hands facing downward. Take a few moments to breathe, relax, clear, and open your minds. As you breathe, begin to establish and energize a sense of your center of energy, awareness, and heartfulness. Using your breathing, begin to extend a field or sphere of these feelings and vibrations around you, and let it reach out to your partner. Simultaneously sense and allow the field and presence of your partner to be ever more deeply within and around you. Allow your fields of luminously charged awareness to blend into a field of sympathetic and harmonious resonance, as though your two notes were reaching out to attune and merge into a dynamic chord of shared awareness.

2. Breath Synchrony

Take turns bringing your attention to the rhythm of your partner's breathing as she or he sits quietly in meditation. Gradually, allow yourself to come into synch with your partner's breathing, and move into a state of sympathetic resonance and empathy. After a while shift, and allow your partner to attune to the natural rhythm of your breath in a similar way.

Finally, simultaneously bring your attention to each other's breathing. Gradually allow your rhythms of inhaling and exhaling to synchronize and flow harmoniously together. Let this shared attunement bring you into greater harmony and understanding at deeper and deeper levels.

3. Giving and Receiving

Another variation on this theme is to alternate inhalations and exhalations with your partner. Imagine breathing out love, energy, light, or healing energy to your partner, who breathes it in. As you inhale, allow yourself to receive whatever quality of heart or mind they offer you. Let this method teach you about how you can open your heart and mind to both give and receive more generously.

4. Merging Hearts and Minds

Begin by sitting across from someone for whom you feel a deep caring and with whom you have a deep bond of love and trust. As you sit here together in a balanced, comfortable way, begin to notice and sense the form, denseness, and solidity of your own body. Now see your partner as an embodied being like yourself, who also has a sensitive, material body that has mass, form, and density. If you like, reach out, hold or touch each other's hands. As you do, feel how the substance of your body meets, greets, and communicates with the substance of your partner's body. As you sit here together, notice how your bodies rest upon and are supported by the forms and structures of the world.

After a while, shift your attention to a more subtle level. Sense that within these dense and solid bodies are more subtle bodies composed of movement, vibration, light, or energy. The vibrancy of these bodies of energy and light pervades your entire physical body and radiates out beyond your skin as warmth, smell, and luminosity into the space around you. As you sense or imagine this natural radiance, let any tension dissolve. Allow your energy to find a natural balance and equilibrium that brings both you and your partner into a peaceful state of natural ease. As you do this, let your awareness reach out and sense your partner as a similarly vibrant and luminous being. Sense or imagine how the natural radiance of your energies reach out, flowing, dancing, and merging together into a larger field. Sense the measurable electromagnetic ripples of your pulsing hearts resounding out through the space that joins you like the circles of two stones dropped side by side into a pool of still water.

Next, shift your awareness to an even subtler level of perception: Within you is an open spaciousness that is deep and clear like a boundless inner sky. Within this inner space all your thoughts, feelings, and energies are free to come and flow. Sense that this inner open space is continuous with the space surrounding you and with the deep inner knowing space of your partner. Let yourself feel the deep, inner quiet and balance of touching this inner spaciousness. Keep in mind that these are actual dimensions of your being. They may already be familiar and known to you, or they may be waiting to be discovered and lifted to the level of conscious awareness.

Resting here in balance and harmony together, sense and imagine the many ways your physical bodies can touch and connect. Notice how the fields and flows of energy and vibration allow you to communicate the energy of love and the resonance and dissonance of emotions. Discover how, in the dimension of your openness, you are of one essence, interpenetrating and sharing an open space of mind.

Now within this matrix of form, energy, and space, establish a nucleus or center of deep love and radiant positive regard. Reach out from this center with a gentle touch or physical caress. At the level of vibration, reach out with a kind word and a warm, luminous wave of love and caring. Sense or imagine a deep and intimate connection as energy flows within and between you. Sense or imagine that in a deep and loving way, the spheres of your energy and awareness can actually merge and interpenetrate, even though your physical bodies occupy distinct and separate spaces.

Allow your fields to become completely shared—open to the flow of unspoken yet profoundly intimate communication springing from the depths of your hearts and minds. From your hearts, fill each other with love and radiate this love to and through each other and to the world. Heart opening to heart opening—marvel at the many dimensions of life you share.

After a while, let your breath gradually bring you back to focus your awareness within the matrix of form-energy-space that is uniquely yourself. Resting here in balance, wonder, and joy, rejoice in the deep, intimate experience of unity and wholeness you have shared.

Merging hearts and minds in this way is also an excellent meditation for extending healing love to a loved one who may be far away. As you bring more attention to the dynamic interplay of form, energy, and openness in your life, you will learn to intimately sense and integrate these three dimensions of aliveness within you, and this inner wisdom will transform the quality of your relationships at their core.

5. Re-Cognizing Each Other
   Sit quietly across from someone you know or love. Like barbershop mirrors deeply reflecting each other, see in one another your parents, grandparents, and ancestors. See too the generational cascade of traditions, attitudes, beliefs, customs, and habits that help or harm. See in yourself, and in each other, the miraculous moment of your conception. See yourselves swimming in the womb of your mothers. See yourselves as tiny children, wide-eyed in a wonder-full world. See in yourself and in each other the potential for becoming a wise old man, a wise old woman. See in yourselves the seeds of influence that will bear fruit in the lives of others for countless generations to come.

Quietly, connectedly, come into harmony within this place where your two streams of being meet. Find balance and common ground together by sharing your visions and by talking about your hopes and fears. Share your life's greatest joys and your sorrows, remembering and learning from the breakdowns and breakthroughs in your lives. Through self-reflection, heartfelt listening, loving inquiry, and mutual understanding, move deeper in relationship toward the dynamic balance that is nourished by opening your hearts to embrace the whole world.

In relationships, people often focus on the amount of time they share together even though the quality of that time may be at best superficial. Often we monitor the health of our relationships by how often we see each other, how many calls we make a week or how many e-mails we send, by how often we make love, or how many evenings a week we are home for supper with our family. All these measures may be significant, yet they are still insufficient for a relationship to really be fully in balance. To develop and maintain a deep and balanced relationship we need to also cultivate a deeper bond of love. If this love is strong, our relationship can be on very solid ground even though we may actually have little time together. It is this inner connection, this bond of love, deep caring, and commitment, that gives true strength to a relationship. Even though you are doing all the right things superficially on the outside, if you aren't developing and strengthening your inner bond the outer connection will lack the strength and deep integrity neces-

sary to endure in a truly nourishing and fulfilling way.

During a yearlong retreat in 1988, we lived in
separate rooms and had very little contact with each
other. Other than an occasional hug on the way to
the dining room, we had no physical contact and
had only a few hours worth of conversation during
the entire year. Yet each day at five o'clock in the
afternoon, we would shift our attention from the
contemplations that were the focus of our retreat
and hold each other in heart and mind. Merging
together like two spheres of light, we would rest in
the light of each other's love as if we were two
beings sharing one heart and looking out through
each other's eyes. It was often a deeply moving and
affirming connection that left us both uplifted and
amazed. Honestly, looking back at the depth of connection we felt with each other, it was strangely the
most intimate year of our lives together.

Nowadays when we are physically apart, traveling on business, we continue to set a time each
day to sit together and link up heart to heart.
During this time, we reach out to each other from
our hearts and let ourselves merge to share a common heart and core. Resting in a state of deep connectedness, in the radiance of our love, we let the
light of our love for each other reach out to others
as an offering and a prayer that will strengthen
them in whatever they need at that time.

Even though we may be some distance apart or
away from each other for some time, when we come
back together we feel closer than ever before. When
we are home or traveling together, we also take

some time to sit quietly together in this way and carry this sense of deep connectedness into our busy days and work in the world. Many people we work with have taken this example to heart and have developed a similar practice they share with their partners. The results are always inspiring.

TRANSFORMING ENERGY:
THE BREATH OF COMPASSION

Wisdom tells me I am nothing. Love tells me I am everything. And between the two my life flows.

—Nisargadatta Maharaj

Of all the meditations for healing we know of, this meditation of energy transformation is without equal in its universally practical applications. Its power lies in reaffirming our dynamic interrelationship with all of life, awakening our generative capabilities, and activating a genuine heartfelt concern for the well-being of others.

The first time we encountered this meditation was at a large international conference on energy healing. As we approached the meeting room we began to hear someone chanting in a beautiful, deep tone—slowly, from the heart. The melody sounded ancient, and although we couldn't understand the words, it stirred the depths of our souls. The workshop leader was the Tibetan lama Geshe Gyaltsen, and the prayer he was chanting accompanied one of the most profound healing and balancing meditations of his tradition. In Tibetan, the name of this meditation for transforming energy is called tong-len, which means "taking and sending." We soon learned that it was one of the most profound meditations we would ever experience.

The practice works by reconnecting us to a larger field of relationship and a vaster sense of ourselves. Often we get out of balance and experience pain and suffering because we've become fixated and overly preoccupied with our own contracted, narrow view. When we are physically, emotionally, or mentally suffering, there is a strong tendency to withdraw from the world and to implode into a very self-centered and self-protective state. We lose perspective of the larger picture and identify too much with the melodramas we are immersed in at the time. This contraction cuts us off from the very healing and balancing energies that we are actually most in need of. The greater our sense of isolation, the greater our suffering, because self-isolation cuts us off from the flow of healing energies that are available to us. The prayer the lama was chanting poignantly depicted this predicament and, out of compassion, called for a transformation of this painful habit of narrow self-focus.

The practice of the following meditation helps build our capacity to transform every experience we may have into an affirmation of loving concern for ourselves, others, and the world. The beautiful paradox is that in opening our hearts beyond our own limited sense of well-being, we also receive benefit ourselves! In the very moment when we generate and extend a genuine energy-wave of loving concern for the well-being and happiness of others, our compassionate attitude produces an immediate effect of healing and blessing within our own minds and bodies at the same time. Although the melodious tones of the lama's chant definitely facilitated the opening and softening process, this meditation works effectively on its own and is complete in itself.

To begin, breathe gently and mindfully for a few minutes, simply noticing the rhythmic movements of your chest or abdomen rising and falling in resonance with your inhalations and exhalations. Allow the area of your chest around your heart center to relax, open, and soften, and establish a clear sense of your inner spaciousness, like a vast open sky. Imagine or feel yourself as hollow and empty inside of all dense or solid organs, like a big body balloon! Totally open and pervaded with light, there is nowhere for anything to lodge. The space within you is continuous with the space outside you. It is as though all the pores of your body are totally permeable to the flow of air and currents of energy that pass in and out of you, and you feel as if you can breathe in and out of all of your pores. (Also see the Hollow Body Meditation, p. 158, for further guidelines on doing this visualization.)

Pause and rest here until you can clearly establish this feeling of open, unobstructed, inner spaciousness.

Then, in the region of your heart chakra, in the center of your chest, imagine a transformational vortex. You might visualize this as a volcanic fire of wisdom burning away the dross of illusions, a black hole in space, a chunk of coal that transforms into a brilliant diamond, a crystalline matrix, or any other metaphor of transformation that suggests itself to you.

Now comes the part of the meditation that Geshe Gyaltsen called, "Hoover vacuum cleaner meditation"! Using the power of your inhalation to work like a vacuum suction, gather up and draw into this transformational vortex any pain or negativity that might be present in your physical, mental, emotional, or spiritual continuum. If you don't feel any particular discomfort anywhere at the present moment, let your inhalation draw in any seeds or latencies that may be lying dormant—potential causes of future suffering that could ripen if conditions became right. You can envision these as heavy, hot energy or dark smoke.

With the motivation of compassion—the desire to reduce or remove suffering—as you inhale, imagine drawing any of these negative energies or potentialities into this vortex . . . and just as the darkness in a room disappears completely and immediately the moment the light is turned on, imagine that the negative energy is completely dissolved and transformed. Instantly, the dark lump of coal is transformed into a sparkling diamond . . . the fire blazes more brightly . . . the black hole of self-absorption turns into a white orb of radiance . . . and the limited sense of yourself is consumed and transmuted into a reservoir of limitless healing power and creativity.

Now, as you exhale, imagine that from your heart center waves of clear, radiant healing light pour forth. Imagine these waves filling your whole body and mind, healing, energizing, and transforming you. Allow the vortex at your heart to function as an energy transformer drawing in negativity, darkness, or pain and transforming it into radiant light and healing energy. For example, drawing in agitation, radiate peace; drawing in anger, radiate patience and compassion. If you take in the suffering of fear with your in-breath, now send back faith with your out-breath. If the pain you breathe in is tension, breathe back relaxation, and so on. "Breathing in hot and heavy . . . breathing out cool and light. . . . " With each exhalation send a wave of healing, balancing energy or influence mounted on the out-breath to whatever region of your body or mind calls for transformation. Some people find it helpful to visualize a color, texture, image, or sound that carries the feeling of the quality they are sending. Others prefer to simply ripple out a clear wave of intention. The key is to allow each breath to deepen and affirm your energetic nature and transformational capabilities.

Continue in this way, sweeping and vacuuming, removing and transforming on the waves of the breath, as long as you like or are able to. Remember to keep your breathing gentle and natural, neither forcing nor holding the breath in any way. As you practice, you may find that the grosser, more noticeable discomforts dissolve or change. When this happens, allow your awareness to be drawn to subtler messages that call for your attention.

The true healing power of this meditation really becomes activated when you begin to understand that the radius of your transformational influence can be vast in its scope, and that you are able to receive and transform the energies of others in the world around you. The larger the field of interrelationship you acknowledge and participate in, the greater will be the reservoir of healing energies you will tap into.

At this level of practice you realize that just as you wish to be free of the pain in your back, your loneliness, or heartache, so too does the person in the seat or house, village or office, next to you. And you also realize that it really doesn't take any extra effort at all as you breathe in to hold the intention to transform the subtle energy of their pain at the same time as you're breathing in and transforming your own.

If you are tormented by anger or grief, imagine and affirm that as you transform these energies or feelings within your own life, those same feelings shared by others are transformed as well. Envision and affirm that a radiance of healing energies emanates out through you to be received by anyone who shares the same feelings. Whatever the form of your distress, use it to affirm the universality of your humanity and your relationship to countless others who share the same feelings or concerns.

When you're ready, reach out with your heart to someone else, to a loved one, a stranger in a hospital bed, or a whole group of people in pain. As you breathe in, draw in their restlessness or frustration along with your own. Offer this energy with compassion to explode the nucleus of separateness and the "small me" consciousness at your heart. And with all the "special effects" you can muster, allow that negative energy to be transformed into its opposite. Send back waves of peace, patience, and radiant light. Experience the openness and connectedness that come as you expand the radius of your active compassion and caring in this way.

Continue as long as you like or have time for, allowing each cycle of breaths to further deepen and affirm your energetic nature and transformational capacity. This is a meditation you can do anywhere, under any circumstances. First start with yourself, then let the circle of your compassionate awareness reach out to others yearning for the same quality of inner and outer harmony that you're looking for.

Practice this method quietly and invisibly—driving or waiting for a bus; during a particularly tense or boring meeting; while watching the evening news; or walking your dog through your neighborhood. This meditation is designed for engagement—an active way of transforming negativity and bringing peace and healing into the world. We regularly practice it when we pull into a hospital parking lot to visit a patient, or while going to work. We've found the healing process begins before we even get into the elevator and serves especially to balance the mind we're bringing in with us! We've taught this practice to tens of thousands of people from all walks of life and from different philosophical and spiritual inclinations. For some, this practice makes immediate, intuitive sense from what they know of the unobstructed flow of energy and information in the natural world. Others translate this practice into a deeply personal participation in Christ's love extending into the world. We invite you to practice it in your own way and see how it speaks to and through you.

Keep in mind that actually being able to visibly transform the negativities of the world through this meditation is secondary to transforming the illusion of your own sense of separateness. The real power of this practice lies in developing a deeper experience of kinship with the world and helping us break free from our preoccupation with our own personal situation. This meditation is essentially a mind training that empowers your inner access to an immense source of transformational potential. It also teaches you to honor and deeply respect the sacred mystery of interdependence by seeing how activating compassion for others works simultaneously to heal your relationship with yourself. Taken to heart, each breath becomes a gesture of relatedness and caring, affirming our wholeness and freeing us from the illusion of separation.

GROUP MEDITATION: ALL MY RELATIONS

Moment by moment, day by day, the practice of meditation is found through living, loving, and learning in the context of "right relations." Interrelationships are the very fabric of the wholeness that embraces all things. We would like to honor the spirit of community by closing with a group meditation practice. We have found this practice to be a wonderful way to acknowledge our deep connectedness and create a shared sacred space—a way to bring a circle of diverse people into harmony with each other and to generate a sense of the humanity and purpose we share in common.

Through the inspiration and blessings of some of our teachers, we have woven this theme into a simple yet potent ritual that is useful to help a group of people focus and connect together in a short time. Many people have shared it with their families at Thanksgiving or at other family gatherings. We sometimes use it to begin a business or community meeting as a reminder of the many people in our families or the stakeholders whose presence needs to be remembered, whose voices we represent, or who will be impacted by our work and our decisions. Often this meditation provides an inspiring way to begin and/or to conclude a workshop, wedding, or service. We have found this simple process useful in many different settings. The key is to create an appropriate context for the practice to have meaning and value for the people who will share it. Here is one way to introduce this meditation:

Sitting in a circle together, we each sense ourselves sitting at the center of our universe surrounded by a boundless circle of all living beings. Reaching out to each other, we join hands. If you are the leader, begin the meditation by saying "all my relations" and give a little squeeze with your left hand to the person on your left. When the person next to you hears you speak and feels the squeeze of your hand, she or he repeats the phrase "all my relations" and squeezes the hand of the next person to the left. Allow the pulse of voices and gentle squeezes to cascade around the circle swiftly and fluidly. Each time we hear or say this phrase, our hearts, minds, and hands reach out to remember and affirm the many people and creatures with whom we are related. We remember the presence of those we love and those who remind us to love more. We remember the presence in our lives of our ancestors and the generations to come, of the humans and non-humans, the seen and unseen beings. All are remembered, as is the inspiring Source of all beings.

If you like, you can invite people to say the name of a loved one or friend, or a group of people or living creatures, whose presence they would like to be remembered in the circle. For example, you might hear: "my children—all my relations," "all the children of the world—all my relations," "my parents—all my relations," "all my students and patients—all my relations," "my friend who is sick—all my relations," "all those who are suffering or lonely—all my relations," "all the people living in fear or in the midst of conflict—all my relations," or "all my grandfathers and grandmothers—all my relations." Allow the energy and pulse of your words to travel round and round the circle, inviting you to remember that our lives have meaning only through kinship with all living beings. Finally, after however many rounds seem right for your group or timeframe—when the pulse returns to the first person who spoke, conclude by inviting everyone to say responsively or all together: "All my relations, let us join together, and as one heart and one mind, give thanks."

When you close, invite people to take a few quiet moments to feel the hands they hold, to sense the presence of everyone in the circle, and to savor the peace, balance, and connectedness that has emerged through this shared contemplation. This may involve simply sitting quietly and feeling the afterglow of the meditation, silently resting in the sense of receiving and radiating blessings to and from all beings, or simply breathing with all beings. If you like, invite people to draw from this boundless network of "all our relations" the inspiring strength, healing energy, or blessings they most need at this time. Draw in inspiration to renew yourself, to release old habits that no longer serve, or to receive and radiate whatever strength, gifts, or prayers you have for others.

This group meditation practice belongs to several of the categories of meditation described in this book. Primarily a heart-centered practice, it also functions as a receptive, mindful listening meditation as well as a concentrative, mantra-like focusing practice—especially if you keep your eyes softly closed and follow the flow of voices around the circle with fluid awareness and careful attention. Heart open, listening to the one song that sings through many voices, reach out and connect in all your dimensions through time and space, taking refuge in this vast network of support and inspiration.

EIGHT
THE PRACTICE OF DEDICATION

CONTINUITY IS THE KEY

ON THE PATH OF SPIRITUAL DEVELOPMENT, dedication and continuity of practice are essential. For millennia, daily meditation or worship, observance of the Sabbath, times of pilgrimage, vision quest, or contemplative retreat have been integral ways of life for people and cultures to stay tapped into the wellsprings of inspiration that continually revitalize and give clear direction to their lives.

Though there is some advantage in doing meditation practice now and then, the real benefits come through establishing the discipline and momentum of daily practice. This is analogous with physical training: intermittent exercise may feel good on occasion, but does little to really develop strength, health, or vitality. Similarly, sporadic meditation practice may feel good but offers little benefit in comparison to daily practice. An ongoing meditation practice increases the power of your presence and the focus of your attention, and strengthens your spirit. Over time, sustained practice literally rewires and increases the capacity of our nervous system. This is quite amazing to see! Developing the discipline and momentum of an ongoing meditation practice can help you to generate the inner strength, resilience, self-confidence, insight, and faith necessary to support you during difficult times. Without such discipline, every time you begin again is like starting from scratch, with little foundation or momentum to draw upon.

Though quality attention is important for the actual time of your meditation, remember that the real goal of meditation practice is to develop a quality of lucid, loving, peaceful, radiant presence that you can then carry over into every moment and activity of your life. Each brief period of quiet meditation to touch and develop your latent strengths and positive qualities concludes with the challenge of carrying these qualities into dynamic action as you set forth to move through the world. Throughout the day, consciously recall and reenergize the feelings of peace, clarity, understanding, kindness, and vitality that you brought alive in your meditation. Particularly when you start to rush and tumble, internally pause, center, and move toward the sense of harmony you experienced earlier in your meditation session. Formal meditation time is really just an opportunity to practice, without distraction, bringing alive those qualities and ways of being you hope to awaken more fully in the other moments of your day.

WEAVING MEDITATION INTO YOUR DAILY LIFE

Periods of quiet, undistracted meditation provide precious opportunities to get in touch with qualities that will gradually grow through cultivation and pervade even your busiest activities. With practice you will find that any activity can become an opportunity to train your mind, develop concentration, refine your awareness, deepen your insight, practice patience or loving-kindness.

There are many simple ways to weave meditation practice into your daily life. For example, we know a woman who does the nine-part breath every morning to help her get focused for the day while she is waiting for her car to warm up. Another friend makes it a daily ritual to watch the sun come up and to contemplate his life in relationship to the cosmos. Others take time each day for contemplative prayer. Many friends practice mindful walking on their way to work. For others, reading or listening to the morning news and opening their hearts to send healing prayers to those suffering throughout the world is a daily form of meditation. Some people practice mindfulness of breathing to polish their minds, or mindfully watch the spontaneous display of the mind's amazing creativity.

Because mindlessness and distraction are such well-established habits, any movement toward developing a meditation practice is a step in the right direction. Many people tell us that they don't feel they have the time to add meditation to the long list of duties already crowding their daily life. As a starting point, we suggest that you experiment with simply being mindful as you do something you regularly do every day, or something that you enjoy. For instance, if you like to walk, walk mindfully. If you like to listen to music, then give yourself time to really listen to some music. If you like to take showers or bubble baths, then bathe mindfully. Or, as you talk with someone that you love, read a story to your child, or make love with your lover, really be there wholeheartedly in the experience.

Properly understood, every activity and every moment of the day offers an invitation to open the door of your heart-mind to a deeper quality of aliveness, relationship, and inspiration. Simple things—brushing your teeth, walking to your office, or mindfully tasting and chewing the first three mouthfuls of food at each meal—can become opportunities to strengthen your mindfulness, build your concentration, or deepen your insight. Stoplights can provide an opportunity to center yourself by consciously enjoying three mindful breaths. Some people find it helpful to practice loving-kindness meditation on the way to work, radiating wishes of peace, happiness, health, and protection to all the drivers rushing headlong around them. Others recite mantras or prayers to steady and anchor themselves in a deeper rhythm as they drive or walk to work. For some of us, a morning meditation may simply be the practice of mindful shaving, mindful make-up application, or mindfully eating breakfast before launching into a busy day. If you work out in the mornings, try building in an extra five to twenty minutes at the end of your workout for deep relaxation and meditation. The natural physiological rebound into deep relaxation after exercise can also be an especially good time to deeply relax and meditate—whatever the time of day. Even the dozens of conversations and interactions you have with people throughout the day can become opportunities to practice deep listening and mindful speaking. If you transform only a few encounters throughout the day with a meditative quality of presence, this will still be quite revolutionary. See how many of the mindless moments of your day can be transformed into opportunities to strengthen concentration, develop mindfulness, deepen insight, expand creativity, and open your heart. Live in a creative and meditative way, as though your life were a dream within which you are awakening.

ORCHESTRATING YOUR MEDITATION PRACTICE

Some meditation practices are like playing a single note, and seeking to make it so pure and clear that we discover the richness of infinite harmonics and overtones within it. Other meditation practices are more complex, like playing a chord, a short tune, or even a whole symphony.

Just as a symphony is comprised of many different movements—each of which is written to carry the listener into a different mood or state of sensitivity—many of the most effective meditation practices are also orchestrated to weave together a number of shorter meditations that could each be taken as a complete practice of meditation unto itself. Examples of such complex meditations can be found in analyses of the Catholic Mass, Hindu *pujas,* and Buddhist *sadhanas.* The daily cycle of prayers and meditations in many great religious traditions offer examples of how such sequences of contemplations may be woven together into a way of life that is a profound and inspiring celebration of spirit and deep awareness.

As you become more familiar with various practices of meditation, choose the techniques that best suit your temperament and natural inclinations. Remember that each technique is an antidote to a particular difficulty and a means of strengthening certain qualities of mind. Trust your heart and your intuitive sense of what you need, but also understand the value of being guided by an experienced teacher.

FINDING A TEACHER

The most effective way to learn anything is to study with someone who has already mastered it. Meditation is certainly no exception. Our mind can be compared to a remarkable musical instrument that is capable of generating the sweetest of music, yet it is often poorly tuned and plagued with chaotic and noisy sounds. If we sincerely wish to learn to play beautiful music, it is helpful to study with a master who knows the instrument inside and out. In order to develop a clear, calm, joyful, and loving mind, we need the guidance of someone who thoroughly understands how the mind works and how it can be transformed . . . someone whose own heart is truly open.

How do you find a qualified teacher? It is not always easy. The qualities to look for in a teacher include compassion, knowledge and insight, morality, sincerity, and skill—both in their teaching and in the way they live their life. For your part, you should have confidence in your teacher and be able to communicate well with him or her. However, don't set out on a frantic guru hunt! Take it easy. It may be a matter of years before you meet the person who can answer your questions and be a spiritual guide for you.

Meanwhile, you can practice meditations such as those described here and seek the advice of any meditators whose qualities you admire. Learn to trust your own intuitive wisdom, your own inner guru, to tell you whether you are heading toward or away from your goal.

SHARPENING YOUR WISDOM OF DISCERNMENT

There are many perils on the path of meditation and spiritual growth. Keep your eyes open and your discerning wisdom keen. There are teachers and traditions that are rare and precious beyond belief. If you are fortunate enough to be able to spend time with them, your life will be truly enriched. There are also teachers and traditions that, quite honestly, we cannot in good conscience recommend. A classic Buddhist teaching advises the spiritual seeker to "First rely on the principle, not on the person. Second, rely on the spirit, not the letter. Third, rely on wisdom, not dogma. And fourth, rely on complete teaching, not incomplete teaching."

How can you know if you are pursuing an authentic spiritual path, or have met a good teacher? Look for the following important indicators: ethical integrity; service to others; compassion; respect for discipline; personal accountability of both leaders and community members; faith; embodiment; groundedness; respect; joyfulness; fellowship with, or at least tolerance for, people of different faiths; an inspiring lineage of practitioners whose lives have been enriched through the practice; a community of kindred souls that inspires your respect and admiration; love; celebration; humanity; respect for silence as well as questions; an honoring of the mythical and the mystical; a path of clear reasoning that welcomes questioning and debate; a balance of prayer, contemplation, study, and service in practice.

If you find that you are easily confused or bewildered by exploring many paths or studying with many teachers, it may be wise to simplify your spiritual pursuits. If diversity overwhelms you, do research until you find a path that is spiritually satisfying for you, and then through study, practice, and contemplation, go deeply into the heart of your chosen path.

If you are by nature a weaver and synthesizer, your temperament may better suit you to seek inspiration from study and practice with a diversity of different traditions. Seek to find the common heart and core around which they come together, and appreciate how each contributes to deepening your wisdom and love and strengthening your faith.

If you are a mature practitioner with a clear sense of your path and tradition, there is little to fear and much to gain through encounters with other traditions. These will likely serve to only clarify and deepen your faith and insight. Keep an open heart, an open mind, and seek for a path that works for you.

Spiritual communities, though potential havens, can also become escapes for the socially challenged. And teachers from other cultures, though masters in their spiritual disciplines, may lack essential experience of their new culture needed to give realistic counsel to students—and sometimes they, too, get distracted as they encounter the enticements of the West.

We wholeheartedly encourage you to keep your eyes wide open. Open-minded skepticism will help you find a healthy balance between overly critical cynicism that may cause you to miss the real thing, and gullible naiveté that will let you be easily duped into signing up for misleading or dangerous pursuits.

Over the years of our search for deeper understanding, our work, travels, and research have led us to encounter many different spiritual paths. Having also encountered many of the perils of the path—and having worked clinically with some of the casualties—we offer the following list of cautionary guidelines to check out before you "sign up" with any spiritual teacher or group. Though it is possible you may also find some of these warning signs on an authentic path, they are more often associated with less trustworthy situations. It is always wise to observe the integrity of people's behavior carefully, and ask yourself:

- Does what I hear make sense to me?
- What is the intention? Is it to harm or to help? Is it for limited self-interest—"self"-improvement—or is it an expression of kindness and service for the good of the whole and of benefit to many for generations to come?

When looking for a spiritually healthy path, beware of any of the following "red flags":

- Teachers or circles of practitioners on your journey who are out of integrity, or who don't practice what they preach.

- Situations where questions are not welcomed or answered in straightforward ways, or where raising concerns about conduct or ethical violations is frowned upon—especially if you are told you are being "too judgmental" when raising honest concerns.

- Anyone who claims that they can give "it" to you, especially for a price.

- Anyone who claims to be the only teacher or path that can deliver the goods.

- If the price of admission excludes people who are truly sincere.

- If you are expected to purchase lots of expensive merchandise or paraphernalia to get on board.

- Slick, extravagant trappings or heavily marketed, empire-building enterprises.

- Discrimination or attempts to turn your heart against others.

- Hidden agendas.

- Fanatical, narrow-minded sects.

- A heavily authoritarian, paternalistic, sexist, or militaristic tone.

- Practices that work with intense energy manipulation or heavy breathing practices that are given without first having established a strong foundation in ethics and personal grounding.

- Teachers, paths, or seminars that seem ungrounded, make outrageous claims, use coercion tactics, or hustle you to get others to sign up.

Be discerning if you encounter people who seem to display unusual or extraordinary powers. People easily confuse psychic sensitivity with spiritual maturity, deluding themselves and others. Channeling, clairvoyance, or other entertaining displays may have little to do with anything spiritual. With teachers who claim to channel disembodied beings, enjoy the show and see if there are any messages of value to you. When in doubt, use common sense and, if you stay around, carefully observe the ethical integrity and behavior of your traveling companions. Because some teachers misrepresent themselves, claiming false spiritual authority, realization, or outright lying about their backgrounds, you may want to check references or question their authenticity. If the biography of a spiritual teacher heavily emphasizes their attainments in past lives, we suggest that you stay focused on the integrity of the one you can see sitting in front of you.

COMMUNITIES OF SUPPORT

Most people find that to maintain the discipline and momentum of a meditation practice it is helpful to have the support of others. Many participate in weekly meditation groups, others in Bible study and prayer groups, while some join book clubs to read and discuss books on meditation, spiritual practice, or peak performance. Others meet with kindred souls at work to take tai chi or yoga classes, or even go for a mindful walk or jog.

Some people choose to live in or near spiritual communities that study the scriptures, do meditation or prayer practice together, or participate in community service projects. In most cities it is possible to find at least one group to meditate with just about any evening of the week. Most groups are open to new people, and few charge a fee. Many groups also meet in the mornings before work, offering wonderful opportunities for fellowship, community practice and support as you start the day.

Since there are so many traditions and styles of meditation practice, it is sometimes helpful to ask friends with more experience which groups they would recommend—and also, perhaps, which to avoid. This process is a bit like finding a new church or synagogue in a new community—it may take a few visits to find a congregation that feels right to you. Also, keep in mind that many more traditional churches, parishes, temples, or synagogues now offer programs on meditation or contemplative prayer. If you are more comfortable with a traditional Judeo-Christian, or New-Thought, approach to meditation, this may be a good place to begin.

Muster the courage to explore some new territory, and "shop around" until you find a group to practice or study with whose community, meditation practice, and style suit your needs. We suggest you rely on the guidance of people whom you respect, and approach this "field research" of local resources with the curiosity, openness, and discernment of an anthropologist or sociologist. It is likely that along the way you will encounter some situations that just don't feel right for you. Keep in mind the "perils of the path" outlined above, and mark those experiences up to learning. Remember, you have no obligation to get involved in any situation that compromises your sense of what is correct for you.

Another way to find a meditation group is to start one! One group we were connected with began with two friends meeting together after work to meditate and share dinner one evening a week. Gradually other friends asked if they could join the circle, and eventually the group grew to over sixty people coming together every week for meditation, followed by a potluck, discussion of themes or readings related to meditation, and sometimes a video or audio tape. Spin-offs of the group led to days of mindfulness, moving parties, community service projects, meditation sessions and potlucks in other neighborhoods at different times, and field trips to lectures, retreats, and the establishment of numerous other meditation groups.

Wherever two or more are gathered with sincerity and an openness to learn and support each other for learning in a sacred way, the potential exists for something wonderful to awaken. So even if you just get together with a friend once a week to talk about your study and practice of meditation, this can be a very powerful support for maintaining the continuity necessary to really deepen your practice.

MEASURING YOUR PROGRESS

How do we know if our practice is a real practice?
Only by one thing: more and more, we just see the
wonder. What is the wonder? I don't know.
We can't know such things through thinking.
But we always know it when it's there.

—Charlotte Joko Beck

Progress in meditation has little to do with unusual or extraordinary experiences in meditation practice. The real fruits of meditation are found in the quality of our daily life and interactions with others. As your wisdom and faith deepen, your genuineness and authenticity will grow, and you'll become more open and sensitive to others. You will begin to live with greater empathy, respect, patience, kindness, and compassion. Developing more harmonious relationships, you'll come to naturally live a more ethical and moral life, and as you do, you will grow freer of the burdens of tension, fear, anger, resentment, hatred, pride, and jealousy. Gradually, authenticity and inner peace, harmony and balance, will come more alive in your life.

There are both inward and outward signs of progress in meditation. Inner indicators will be reflected by your answers to these questions:

- Are there more moments of mindfulness and fewer moments of mindlessness in your life?
- Is your sense of authenticity growing?
- Are you better able to concentrate and stay focused on what you are doing without distraction or dullness taking over your mind?
- Are you growing kinder and more compassionate toward yourself and others?
- Are you learning to listen better and more deeply— both within and outside yourself?
- Are you more comfortable with being alone and more at ease when you are with others?
- Is your sense of awe, wonder, faith, and reverence growing?

Outer indicators of success in your meditation will be reflected by your responses to these questions:

- Are you more mindfully present with others?
- Are you more aware of what is going on—within and around you?
- Are you naturally becoming more ethical in your relationships with others?
- Are you better able to recognize and suspend your mental models and assumptions in order to look and listen deeply enough to recognize what is really going on?

- Are you becoming more patient, tolerant, and compassionate toward others?
- Are you becoming more sensitive to the intensity of both beauty and suffering in the world around you?

Avoid fascination with transient "peak experiences" and instead be prepared to spend much of your time on the plateau of gradual, often imperceptible, progress, knowing that over time continuity of practice will profoundly transform how you experience yourself and your world.

A DAY OF MINDFUL RETREAT

From time to time it can be helpful to dedicate a longer period of time to deepen your practice of meditation. Setting aside a day, a weekend, or a week can provide a rare and welcome oasis amid the densely packed business of daily life. Since you will likely never "find" the time, we encourage you to *make* the time.

Simplifying your outer life for a day can help you to discover and develop the richness of your inner life. For even just one day, forget that you have a TV, let the phone answer itself, set aside all the e-mail and busywork that tend to gobble up and dominate your time, attention, and life.

Given our busy lifestyles and obligations, taking a day for ourselves can seem like an unreasonable luxury, but if you can arrange it, the time can offer inspiration and value that will enrich the relationships to which you return. Couples can benefit from taking such a retreat together, and in supporting each other in an occasional day of solitary retreat (see guidelines below). So often in everyday life we lose ourselves in our relationships, and it can be very empowering, inspiring, and fulfilling to simply, quietly, be mindfully all-one with yourself for a day of meditation in a relatively undistracted way.

In preparation, make a plan to minimize intrusions and, if time permits, clean up or unclutter your place a bit. For some people it can be helpful to put out some pictures of loved ones or inspiring teachers, or arrange some flowers, candles, and perhaps some music that uplifts your spirits. If by chance visitors stop by, greet them warmly and explain that you are devoting the day to work on a very important project and try to find another time to get together with them.

The first step, as in all meditations, is to set a clear intention for the day. Why is this day important to you? What qualities or strengths do you wish to cultivate and bring more alive during this time? Which specific meditation practices or themes do you intend to focus on during this rare and precious time?

We suggest that you choose one or two meditation practices you have been drawn to, and deepen your practice of them during this day. When in doubt, try to keep it very simple and let this be a day of mindfulness meditation.

Ideally begin each session by affirming your connection to the sources of inspiration that support and inspire you in your practice. (See the Taking Refuge meditation on page 41.)

Then shift your attention to a practice that develops your concentration, such as mindful breathing, the nine-part breath, the elemental purification breaths, or the mindful repetition of a mantra or prayer. Any of these practices will help you develop the calm intensity and presence of mind necessary to stay more focused with whatever meditation practices you choose to work with throughout the day.

Once you have inspired and focused your mind, turn your attention to your chosen meditation practice. Emphasize the quality of attention you are bringing to your practice by starting with short, focused sessions—three to ten minutes at a stretch to begin with. Then mindfully take a very short break—a minute or so—to stretch or mindfully look around, and then once again refocus your attention for the next period of meditation. Continue with short, focused periods of meditation, being vigilant not to slip into dullness or distraction. Don't get too concerned about using a clock or timer for your meditation sessions; simply take a short break to refresh yourself when you notice that the quality of your attention is starting to drift or wane.

After a half-hour to an hour of these short, quiet sitting meditations interspersed with brief breaks, make a smooth and mindful transition into some kind of mindful movement: slow mindful walking, stretching, or even moving or dancing to some music that you enjoy. Keep your awareness anchored in your body—experience your aliveness, the flow and tingle of sensations and vibrations coursing through you. After about twenty to forty-five minutes of mindful moving, return to stillness, inspire and focus your mind, and continue with your quiet meditation practice.

Follow a similar rhythm throughout the day: quiet meditation alternating with moving meditation. When appropriate, drink a mindful cup of tea, or prepare and eat a mindful meal. It may also be helpful to weave some time of inspirational reading and reflection into the day, especially if you are in need of some upliftment. Slow down and continue to maintain a continuity of attention as you move, drink tea, or go to the bathroom. Let every action of this special day be done with mindful tenderness, and a sense of inquiry, discovery, and appreciation.

If during the day you find that mental dullness or heaviness is an obstacle, read something inspirational or contemplate some theme that will uplift your mind, such as gratitude for the precious gifts of your life, or for the beauty of nature. Taking a shower or going for a mindful walk may also help to reenergize you and leave your mind fresh and clear for your meditations. If you find that you are really exhausted, give yourself permission to take a nap, then mindfully resume your practice when you awaken more rested.

If your mind is really agitated and distracted, it may be helpful to practice mindfulness of breathing, the nine-part breath, the elemental breaths, or to recite a mantra to help settle the mind. Sometimes going for a mindful walk in nature, or even a mindful run, can help you burn off some of the agitation and leave you feeling more peaceful and calm, ready for more still and quiet meditation practice.

If possible, watch the rising or setting of the sun and moon, watch the stars come out, and appreciate the wonders of the natural world. A day, weekend, or week of meditation in nature can offer a welcome opportunity to remember your place within the larger circle of life.

Finally, at the end of the day, pause to reflect, write in your journal, and harvest the insights from this rare and precious experience. Reflect on the gifts and lessons of this day, and upon their significance and meaning for how you will live the days of your life to follow. Ask yourself:

- What has been the greatest gift or blessing of this day?
- What has been your greatest challenge today?
- Where today were you surprised?
- Where today were you most deeply moved?
- What inspired you the most today?
- What questions do you end the day with?
- What clear direction or calling has emerged for how you want to live your life in the precious days to come?
- Who do you need to connect with and what are your messages to them?
- What is your heart's prayer as this day comes to an end?

As you mindfully complete your daily rituals and prepare for bed, let your last meditation be one of dedication (see page 243). Take to heart the blessings and gifts of the day and radiate a wave of loving-kindness, compassion, and gratitude, sending ripples of inspiring strength and blessings to share with all beings.

As you move toward sleep, practice the series of sleeping and dreaming meditations (beginning on page 165). And when you awaken in the morning, be mindful of your breathing and set a clear intention to carry the momentum of yesterday's inner work into this new day of possibilities and opportunities.

SHARING YOUR RETREAT WITH OTHERS

The retreat guidelines offered above can easily be expanded to allow for sharing the day with others you may invite to join you. These guidelines can also be extended to any number of days that you wish—a weekend, a week, or even longer.

Sharing a time of meditation retreat with someone else can be a wonderful experience—or a challenging one. If others will be practicing with you, set clear expectations before you begin regarding how you will interact during the retreat. It can be very powerful—and bonding—to silently practice together and to maintain a mindful, joyful silence throughout the day. Sitting together, walking together, cooking and eating together in silence, can be a very profound and mutually supportive experience.

The main point to keep in mind is to support each other through your presence and practice, and not to distract one another with activity or speaking. If you want or need to speak, set a time to check in with each other to see how things are going, or perhaps set a time in the afternoon or evening for mindful dialogue and sharing insights and inspirations. Remember, as always, that your work is on yourself, and the same applies to your companions. Be supportive of each other, but give each other the space to work with and through whatever insights or obstacles arise without having to immediately get involved. If you plan to share a day of mindful meditation with a group of people, it may also be helpful to assign tasks for the day, such as preparing a meal or cleaning up. This can be simplified by having food prepared ahead of time. Sharing days of mindfulness with friends on a regular basis can be a wonderful way to build your practice, deepen relationships, and build a community of support all at the same time.

MEDITATION IS THE PRACTICE OF "DEEP RELATIONSHIP"

Remember, meditation is truly the practice of "deep relationship." By this we mean that even though meditation may appear from the outside to be quite a solitary endeavor, what it opens up for us from the inside, is a profound experience of our deep connectedness to humanity, to other living beings, and to the whole cosmos. Taking this to heart, we realize that we can never practice meditation alone—even if we are in a cave or isolated retreat—because at some level we are always deeply connected to all beings, especially to those with whom we have a strong bond of love and faith. Drawing inspiration from these deep connections can provide a profound source of strength and support for our contemplative practice. As we weave the methods and principles of meditation more deeply into our daily life, they gradually carry us from separation, to deep connection, to a sense of unity and wholeness in which all things and all beings are deeply related.

FAITH AND THE FIVE POWERS

There are five qualities of mind that are crucial for supporting the continuity of your meditation practice. These five principal powers are:

— Factors that build mental power.
— Factors that dissipate mental power.

Classically, self-doubt or lack of faith is considered the greatest obstacle to meditation practice. Faith and self-confidence free us from confusion and doubt, liberating the energy needed to focus the mind and overcome lethargy. When the energy of the mind is focused, it generates the power of concentration, which transforms distraction. When concentration is sustained, mindful attention increases and mindlessness is lessened. As our mindful presence grows, our insight and understanding naturally deepen, giving rise to greater self-confidence and faith. Properly understood and applied, the dynamic interplay of these five powers provides the momentum necessary for your meditation to soar.

DEDICATION MEDITATION

In moments of focused prayer, meditation, kindness, caring, and mindful work, we generate a potency, like an electrical charge, within the stream of our being. Like sweet ambrosia, this vital energy fuels our spiritual evolution. Living a mindful, loving life, the strength and potency of this vitality grows within us, nourishing our soul, body, mind, and relationships. But in moments of mindlessness, fear, negativity, or anger, we bleed off this vitality and deplete ourselves.

Understanding this, a powerful meditation practice, called "dedication," was developed. This is a practice for renewing and building the positive spiritual energy that grows through the wisdom and generosity of the heart. To get a sense for how it works, imagine that as you distill the spiritual ambrosia from your positive actions, you can also put a drop of this sweet nectar into the cup of everyone you love or even into the cup of every being. Your offering carries with it a potency, and becomes a source of nourishment and inspiration in their own lives, inspiring them and deepening their own wisdom and love.

It's as though with each "dividend check" you receive for your good works, you consciously reach out from your heart and dedicate or deposit a little of your own spiritual "capital" into others' "bank accounts." Your investment in them increases their spiritual wealth. Then, if through mindlessness or recklessness you knock over your own cup or dissipate your personal reserves, all is not lost. Through your deep, heartfelt connections with others, there are resources from which you can draw strength and inspiration. In times when your own storehouse may be low or depleted, it is likely that you will be able to receive support from the interest that has accrued due to your previous kindness. In this way, the gains you realize can never be fully destroyed.

In the spirit of dedication, we would like to offer the following heart-centered creative meditation to deepen your understanding of this essential practice. As our teachers would say, this is also an auspicious way to end this book! We invite you to join with us in radiating waves of inspiration and blessings to all who may benefit through what has been offered here, and through what you will bring alive by your own sincere practice of these teachings.

Imagine yourself standing in front of a sacred well. You are parched and yearning to have your thirst quenched. "I am so thirsty," you say, raising your cup up to be filled. "Please fill my cup that I might quench my thirst." Filling your cup with cool, clear water, the responsive and compassionate Universe says, "Here, thanks for asking. May your thirst and wishes be fulfilled." You raise your cup to drink, and the sweet waters quench your thirst, quell your longing, and you feel refreshed.

Having tasted such sweetness, you then look around. So many others are still thirsty. Their cups are broken or empty, their lips are cracked. They too yearn to be fulfilled. Moved by compassion, you return to the sacred well. This time you ask, "Please, will you fill my cup, and while you fill my cup, will you fill the cups of those I love, and the cups of my friends and neighbors? They too are thirsty, they too yearn to have their cups filled and their thirst quenched. It is unbearable to see their pain. Please help them as you have helped me." "Of course," comes the compassionate voice from the wellspring, "May the thirst of all those you care for be quenched and their wishes be fulfilled. Thanks for asking." Raising your cup to drink this second time, you look around delighted to see that the cups of those you love are also filled. It's marvelous! As you drink together this time, the water tastes even sweeter and the satisfaction is so much greater as you sense within you the deep satisfaction of many others. It feels wonderful!

As you approach the well the third time you are smiling. There is a twinkling in your eye. You now understand how this process works. Raising your cup to be filled, this time you say, "My thirst reminds me that all beings thirst for something. As you fill my cup, will you please fill the cups of each being and satisfy whatever their longing and desires are?" "Of course," replies the compassionate voice of the deep well, "May the cups of each being be filled with exactly that which will bring them into peace, harmony, and balance in their lives. May their every wish be fulfilled! Thanks for asking." As the sweet, clear nectar fills your cup again you look around. As far as you can see, as far as you can imagine, near and far, friend and foe, into the past and into the distant future, countless cups are raised and filled. As you drink and the clear nectar fills you with sweet satisfaction, you know that countless desires have been fulfilled, and that each being in their own way has at least a drop more peace and balance in their life because of your generosity of spirit. Your own satisfaction is inexhaustible. A toast to all beings!

Ultimately, you realize that your power of dedication flows from the wellsprings of your own deepest heart. Any time you have an experience of joy, beauty, forgiveness, or love—anytime you meditate, read an inspiring book, practice patience, compassion, or generosity—you can share the positive energy that you've generated, by radiating it directly from your heart into the hearts and souls of all beings, through the practice of dedication.

As we reach the completion of this book, let's now join our hearts and minds together and dedicate all the gifts we've received by closing with a meditative prayer of dedication:

By the power and truth of this practice,
May all beings have happiness and the causes of
    happiness,
May all be free from sorrow and the causes of sorrow,
May all never be separated from the sacred peace and
    joy beyond all sorrow,
May all beings fully awaken to their true nature and
    potentials and be free.

As you practice these holy teachings,
slowly the clouds of sorrow will melt away.
And the sun of wisdom and true joy
will be shining in the clear sky of your mind.

—Kalu Rinpoche

RESOURCES FOR CONTINUED LEARNING

THERE ARE MANY INSPIRING BOOKS, websites, and resources available to help you deepen your study and practice of the methods presented in this book. The sources are too numerous to list in full here so we invite you to visit our website, *www.wisdomatwork.com/meditation*, for a listing of recommended resources.

For information on our other books and recordings, including *Wisdom at Work, Living in Balance, A Moment to Relax, The Fine Arts of Relaxation, Concentration, & Meditation*, etc., please visit: *www.wisdomatwork.com* and click on "Resources and Publications."

AN INVITATION

We welcome your invitations to offer keynotes, workshops, special retreats, or consultations for your community or organization. Please contact us at *levey@wisdomatwork.com*. For information on our workshops and programs that are open to the general public, visit *www.wisdomatwork.com* and *www.kohalasanctuary.com*.

ACKNOWLEDGMENTS

THIS BOOK IS LIKE A LAKE FED BY STREAMS flowing from many sources of inspiration. We are grateful to Mary Jane Ryan, Will Glennon, Nina Lesowitz, Brenda Knight, and all those at Conari Press whose initial vision and dedication to the first edition of this book helped bring it to life. For her belief in this book, her creative counsel, and her patient support in bringing this beautiful new edition to the world, we deeply thank our publisher Jan Johnson and her able staff at Red Wheel/Weiser. To Joan Borysenko, we give our heartfelt appreciation and gratitude for her inspiration, friendship, and the brilliant foreword for this book. Special thanks also go to Jed and Kaoru Share for our photo, to Sheila Hoffman for her illustrations, and to our many colleagues who so kindly offered their endorsements for this book. We likewise extend our heartfelt thanks to our many colleagues, friends, students, and clients who have offered their insights, anecdotes, and inspirations regarding the practical integration of these methods into daily life.

Honoring our first teachers, Joel would like to acknowledge his mother Recia Millar, and grandparents Hilda and Abe Levey, whose faith, courage, discipline, and kindness inspired him to cherish life and to value what he does.

Michelle beams gratitude to her beloved parents, Ida and Benjamin Gold, without whose gifts and examples she would not have set out on her own unique path of learning, practice, and discovery.

Our dance together as co-authors in writing this book has offered countless opportunities for us to put the principles and practices of *Luminous Mind* to the test. We bless and thank each other for the patience and devotion required to write this book, while attending to the myriad projects of our lives and work. Our love and wisdom have deepened on the journey we've shared, receiving and contemplating these teachings, reflecting upon them together, and weaving words through which these illuminating teachings can shine through into your minds, and for all this we are grateful.

Most importantly, we acknowledge our debt of gratitude to those great beings whose teachings and writings have been so crucially instructive and inspirational to us over the past forty years. We have been fortunate to devote our lives to intensive study, practice, and teaching of the world's great modern and ancient wisdom traditions, and have been blessed to receive guidance from many of the most revered contemplative teachers of our times. *Luminous Mind* reflects the illuminating wisdom and extraordinary kindness of our many teachers, including: His Holiness Tenzin Gyatso the XIV Dalai Lama, Kyabje Zong Rinpoche, Kalu Rinpoche, Dipa Ma, Lama Thubten Yeshe, Geshe Dhargye, Gen Lamrimpa, Sogyal Rinpoche, Chagdud Rinpoche, Robert Thurman, Rina Sircar, Brother David Steindl-Rast, David Chetlahe Paladin, Rabbi Shlomo Carlbach, Rabbi Zalman Shachter Shalomi, Faisal Muqquadam, Pir Vilayat Khan, Thich Nhat Hanh, Angeles Arrien, Ram Dass, Paul Reps, Jack Kornfield, S.N. Goenka, Sharon Salzberg, Ruth Dennison, Robert Hover, Kumu Raylene Ha'alalea Lancaster, Stephen & Ondrea Levine, and so many others.

Luminous Mind bridges many worlds and thanks are also due to numerous friends and colleagues in the modern mind-science research community who have inspired our work. These include: Jon Kabat-Zinn, Daniel Goleman, Andy Weil, Richard Davidson, Larry Dossey, Marilyn Schlitz, Rupert Sheldrake, Robert Jahn, Bill Arnesen, Adam Engle, and so many others working selflessly to deepen our understanding of the profound implications and applications of the inner science traditions in our modern lives and times. The unique and profound examples of each of these colleagues and spiritual friends, their skillful methods of teaching, and their patient guidance of our practice have opened our heartminds to live with wonderment, faith, and reverence for the profound Mysteries and potentials of our precious lives and luminous minds.

Holding lineages of teachings that have been cherished for millennia, our teachers have preserved the streams of their transmissions of ancient wisdom into these modern times when such wisdom is at a premium. Each of these great teachers has witnessed or endured tremendous suffering that has opened their hearts and minds to teach with great compassionate wisdom and faith. In recent years, many of these remarkable teachers have passed from this world, leaving us with a rare and precious legacy to nurture, and to share what we have learned with those we meet through our work, writing, and travels. In this spirit, if this book serves to help you to feel a connection with our teachers and with their wisdom lineages, and if it inspires you to practice and realize the illuminating wisdom of these teachings, and then to carry the light of that realization as a source of inspiration and blessing in your life and in the lives of all you meet, then our highest intentions in writing this book will have been amply fulfilled. With the waves of each breath, we invite you to affirm your connection to countless sources of inspiration and to allow your heart to extend this inspiration out to others. Living in this luminous gesture of receiving and radiating is truly the heart essence of this book.

Through the wisdom and kindness of all these and countless other people, the spirit of the profound practices offered in this book has been woven deeply into the fabric of our lives. Now, through your own sincere reflection and practice, may the illuminating spirit of these precious teachings come to life for you, and through you to all whose lives you touch along The Way.

INDEX OF MEDITATION PRACTICES

REFLECTIVE MEDITATION

Photo: jed and kaoru share

ABOUT THE AUTHORS

JOEL LEVEY, PH.D., AND MICHELLE LEVEY, M.A., are founders of InnerWork Technologies, Inc. (*wisdomatwork.com*); The International Center for Contemplative Inquiry; and The International Center for Corporate Culture & Organizational Health. Their pioneering, integral approach to helping individuals, organizations, and communities realize their highest potentials has inspired clients in over 200 leading organizations around the globe, including: World Bank, NASA, Intel, Hewlett-Packard, Washington Athletic Club, MIT, Stanford Research Institute, Indian Institute of Management, and West Point Academy. They steward the Kohala Sanctuary on the Big Island of Hawaii (*kohalasanctuary.com*), where they host transformational retreats and gatherings in the Aloha Spirit. The Leveys have directed mindfulness-based clinical stress mastery programs for Group Health and Children's Medical Center and their work in "Meditation & Integral Medicine" has inspired faculty and students in dozens of medical and nursing schools. Widely published and recognized as leaders in these fields, the Leveys' corporate programs, writings, and public workshops have guided tens of thousands of people worldwide to bring a deeper wisdom, resilience, and compassion to life.

TO OUR READERS

CONARI PRESS, AN IMPRINT OF RED WHEEL/WEISER, publishes books on topics ranging from spirituality, personal growth, and relationships to women's issues, parenting, and social issues. Our mission is to publish quality books that will make a difference in people's lives—how we feel about ourselves and how we relate to one another. We value integrity, compassion, and receptivity, both in the books we publish nad in the way we do business.

Our readers are our most important resource, and we appreciate your input, suggestions, and ideas about what you would like to see published. Please feel free to contact us, to request our latest book catalog, or to be added to our mailing list.

Conari Press
An imprint of Red Wheel/Weiser, LLC
500 Third Street, Suite 230
San Francisco, CA 94107
www.conari.com